The Cambridge Manuals of Science and
Literature

AUSTRALIA

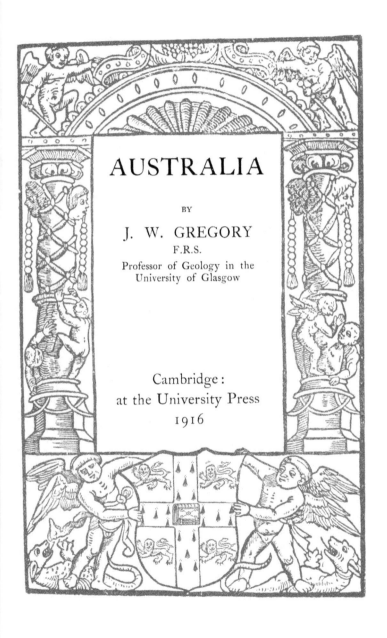

AUSTRALIA

BY

J. W. GREGORY

F.R.S.

Professor of Geology in the
University of Glasgow

Cambridge:
at the University Press
1916

CAMBRIDGE UNIVERSITY PRESS
Cambridge, New York, Melbourne, Madrid, Cape Town,
Singapore, São Paulo, Delhi, Tokyo, Mexico City

Cambridge University Press
The Edinburgh Building, Cambridge CB2 8RU, UK

Published in the United States of America by Cambridge University Press, New York

www.cambridge.org
Information on this title: www.cambridge.org/9781107639409

© Cambridge University Press 1916

First published 1916
First paperback edition 2011

A catalogue record for this publication is available from the British Library

ISBN 978-1-107-63940-9 Paperback

Cambridge University Press has no responsibility for the persistence or
accuracy of URLs for external or third-party internet websites referred to in
this publication, and does not guarantee that any content on such websites is,
or will remain, accurate or appropriate.

*With the exception of the coat of arms at
the foot, the design on the title page is a
reproduction of one used by the earliest known
Cambridge printer, John Siberch, 1521*

PREFACE

THE manuscript of this book was completed on the way home from my fourth visit to Australia in 1914. Its publication has been delayed by the War in which Australia has joined so nobly, and her forces have fought so heroically and successfully. The statistics quoted are not now the latest available, but it has not seemed advisable to alter them since they illustrate the normal conditions of Australia better than those of the last three years.

J. W. G.

October, 1916.

CONTENTS

ILLUSTRATIONS

CHAPTER I

THE DISCOVERY, EXPLORATION AND POPULATION OF AUSTRALIA

The European discovery of Australia began in 1606, when a Dutch vessel, the *Duyfhen*, under the command of a captain whose name is unknown, crossed from New Guinea into the Gulf of Carpentaria and sailed along its eastern shore to Cape Turn-again or Keer-weer. He reported that there was no outlet eastward to the Pacific and this land was therefore regarded as part of New Guinea; for though Torres had previously sailed through Torres Strait, his discoveries were unknown. Hence the existence of an independent land to the south-east of the Malay Archipelago was first recognized when Dirk Hartog, in 1616, sailed along part of the north-western coast of Australia. Other Dutch explorers between that date and 1642 determined the general course of the western coast of Australia. They thus proved the truth of earlier rumours of a great land to the south-east of Java. A great southern continent had been assumed on theoretical grounds by the medieval geographers; and vague reports, probably based on voyages by Malays, led to the representation on the maps of the fifteenth and sixteenth centuries of a vast island in the position of Australia. It was usually known as Jave la Grande, but Wytfliet, who in 1597 said it was so large as to be "a fifth part of the world," called it "Australis Terra."

These early Dutch explorations led up to the famous voyage of Tasman, in 1642. His expedition was despatched by van Diemen, the governor of Java. It discovered Tasmania and New Zealand, and gave the name of New Holland to the Australian continent.

British participation in the exploration of Australia began in 1686 and 1699 with the two voyages of William Dampier. He visited the north-western coast, and saw one of the least attractive parts of the continent; so he returned with unfavourable opinions of both the country and its people. Another seventy years elapsed before the next British explorer reached Australia. Then, in 1770, that greatest of British seamen, Captain Cook, crossed in the *Endeavour* from Tasmania to Victoria and sailed thence along the whole eastern coast of Australia. This epoch making voyage proved that the New Holland of the Dutch extended so far eastward as to be indeed a continent. Cook, and his illustrious companion, Banks, recognized that eastern Australia was a land of greater fertility than the western regions, which

Dampier had described as "the barrenest spot on earth," and which the Dutchman Nuyts condemned as "a foul and barren shore." Cook and Banks were both at first disappointed with the appearance of the country. Banks once referred to it as "the most barren country I have ever seen." Cook described it as "upon the whole rather barren than fertile"; but, he continued, "yet the rising ground is chequered by woods and lawns, and the plains and vallies are in many places covered with herbage"; and he reported the country as well watered. Though Cook and Banks were cautious in their first estimates of the value of Australia, to them is due the beginning of its colonisation. After the loss of the United States the British Government wanted some fresh penal settlement, and Cook and Banks urged that Australia should be used for this purpose. An expedition was sent out under Captain Phillip. It landed in January, 1788, at Botany Bay, the locality recommended by Cook. Port Jackson was at once recognized as a better situation, so the colony was transferred thither, and established on the site of Sydney.

From this centre the exploration of the continent was begun. Lieut. Ball first circumnavigated Australia in 1790, without however conclusively proving its unity. Bass showed that Tasmania was isolated from the mainland by sailing through

1—2

Fig. 1. Sydney Harbour

Bass Strait during a cruise in an open boat from Sydney to Western Port.

After the voyage of Cook the greatest single contribution to knowledge of the Australian coasts was made by Flinders during the voyage of the *Investigator*, 1801–1803. He then discovered the chief geographical features on both the southern and northern coasts and, as Prof. Scott has shown, to him is really due the adoption of Australia as the name of the continent. Flinders surveyed the Great Australian Bight, Spencer Gulf, and the Gulf of Carpentaria. He thus finally disproved the hypothesis that the New South Wales of Cook was separated by sea from the New Holland of the Dutch explorers. The survey of the north-western coasts by King in 1817 and 1822, completed the preliminary examination of the Australian coast.

The inland exploration of Australia was long delayed by the difficulty of finding a practicable route from the coastal plains around Sydney up the steep face of the East Australian Highlands. All the attempts to climb these mountains failed until 1813, when a devastating drought on the coastal plains stimulated more determined efforts to reach the highlands. Three explorers, Wentworth, Blaxland and Lawson, then forced their way up a spur and found themselves on a plateau, which they crossed until the rivers flowed westward into the interior of the continent. The same year an expedition under Evans advanced further into the interior and discovered the Macquarie River; and the same explorer subsequently reached the Lachlan River. It was believed that no great river had its outlet on the southern coast of Australia; so Oxley was sent, in 1815, to trace the Lachlan River to its end. He followed the river until his progress was stopped by wide swamps; and, after another attempt, he concluded that the rivers flowing into the interior down the western slope of the highlands all ended in vast swamps or in an inland sea.

Attention was then diverted from the districts west of Sydney to the south-west. The Murray River was discovered in 1823. It was crossed in 1824–25 by Hume and Hovell, who discovered the snow-clad Australian Alps, and reached the shores of Port Phillip at Geelong. In 1828 Allan Cunningham, the Kew botanist, found a way from Brisbane, through Cunningham's Gap, on to the high plains of southern Queensland, and thus opened the way to the settlement of the rich country known as the Darling Downs. The same year Sturt visited the Macquarie River to determine the conditions of the river basins in the interior of New South Wales during a period of drought. He found that the Macquarie River disappeared on the plains, and that the water in its pools and even in a flowing stream was intensely salt. The party nearly perished of thirst, and Sturt returned with the report that the interior of Australia was a desert watered by rivers of brine. Next year Sturt descended the Murrumbidgee to its junction with the Murray River and continued down it to the sea; but his account of the country he had seen and of the value of the Murray was again discouraging.

A truer estimate however was formed a few years later by Sir Thomas Mitchell, who, in 1835, crossed from Sydney to the upper part of the Darling River, and followed it south-westward nearly to its junction with the Murray. He thus disproved the idea that the Upper Darling discharged to the sea on the northern coast. The following year Mitchell made the most epoch making of all Australian expeditions. He continued his former route south-westward along the Darling, till it flowed into the Murray, and then explored western Victoria; he reached the southern coast at Portland, where he found that the Hentys had established a whaling and sealing station. Thence he returned across western and central Victoria. He was so delighted with the country that he named it "Australia Felix," and his glowing descriptions of its fertility led to its rapid occupation by sheep farmers. Many of them came from Tasmania and entered Victoria through the newly established ports at Melbourne and Geelong.

Melbourne was first occupied in 1835 by a few settlers
from Tasmania. It was proclaimed a town in 1837;
and within ten years of that date most of the fertile
and open plains of Victoria had been occupied as
sheep stations.

The exploration of the middle part of southern
Australia was begun from Adelaide, which was
founded as an experimental colony in 1836. A
grant of land in that region had been awarded to
the South Australian Colonisation Association in
1834; and a party of colonists, organized in accordance with the principles of Gibbon Wakefield and
trusting for revenue to the sale of land, arrived at
the end of 1836. Adelaide was proclaimed a township in 1837. The country between it and Melbourne
was explored by the "Overlanders," who crossed
from Port Phillip with cattle. The most famous
of these men was Eyre, subsequently Governor of
Jamaica. He settled for a while in South Australia,
made the earliest explorations northward from the
head of Spencer Gulf, and discovered that the country
was a desert with vast salt lakes. The country to the
north being then valueless, Eyre turned his attention
westward, and during the most adventurous journey
in Australian annals, marched around the Great
Australian Bight to the settlements on the western
coasts.

The occupation of Western Australia, an area for

which will be adopted the convenient and oft-used abbreviation Westralia[1], had meanwhile been begun in 1829 in order to secure the British possession of the whole of Australia; the colony was for long confined to the Swan River Settlement at Perth and at Albany on the magnificent harbour of King George Sound. Many daring pioneer expeditions organized from Perth returned with most unfavourable reports of the interior; and the better watered districts in the northern part of the territory were too tropical and too remote to tempt extensive settlement at that time. The occurrence of gold in Westralia was first proved in 1848; the existence of a gold-field was first discovered in the northern districts, in Kimberley, by Hardman in 1884; but it was not until 1892, that the first mining discovery of immediate political importance was made at Coolgardie. The search from that gold-field led to the finding of the rich gold mines of Kalgoorlie. Permanent settlements were then established in the interior, and from them prospectors and pastoralists discovered the chief features in the geography of the country. Railways have since been constructed far

---

[1] This term avoids such apparent contradictions as eastern Western Australia or such tautology as western Western Australia, and the ambiguity of the term Western Australia when used for a political division and more indefinitely for the western part of the continent.

inland to serve the widespread mining fields, though with the exception of the mining towns the population is mainly confined to the better watered agricultural districts of the south-western corner of the State.

The first journeys towards central Australia were organized in the hope of finding there a mountainous well-watered country; but after Eyre and Sturt had described the area to the north of the South Australian Highlands as hopeless desert, the main motives of exploration were geographical discovery and the ambition to cross the unknown interior to the opposite coasts. It was found during these journeys that districts which had been described as barren wastes were covered after wet seasons with rich grass and dotted with fresh water lakes.

The first explorers to cross the Continent from south to north were Burke and Wills, both of whom perished beside Cooper Creek in 1861 during their return journey. Macdonald Stuart, working further to the west, after several attempts, succeeded in 1862, in crossing from Adelaide to the coast of the Northern Territory and back again. Leichhardt endeavoured to traverse the continent from east to west, and the complete disappearance of his expedition somewhere to the north of Lake Eyre is one of the great mysteries of Australian exploration, for no trace of his extensive equipment has ever been found. Efforts to discover his fate contributed greatly to knowledge of the interior. Sir A. C. Gregory, when in command of one of the search expeditions, developed the methods of travel with small, lightly equipped parties and showed how the northern interior could be successfully explored.

The colonisation of Australia had been begun in 1788 (cf. p. 3) by the establishment of a penal settlement which consisted of a little over 1000 persons including the convicts and their guard. It should be remembered that at that time most serious crimes received capital punishment, and men were deported for minor offences such as poaching, and for political misdemeanours, such as the establishment of an agricultural trades union. Judged by modern standards many of the prisoners were better men than some of their jailers; and early explorers who worked with parties of the convicts were enthusiastic in their praise. The convicts were never very numerous; none were sent to the colonies of Victoria or South Australia, since they had refused to receive them; the last shipment to Westralia was made in 1867. This element in the population was completely swamped by the great inrush of settlers in 1851 after the discovery of the gold-fields. The main influence in Australia of the penal settlement was indirect, and is to be seen in the trend it gave toward socialistic government.

The total population of the Commonwealth, excluding the aborigines, according to the census of 1911 is 4,455,005 or an average of 1·53 persons per square mile. Australia is therefore the emptiest of all the occupied continents, as Asia, in spite of its vast northern wastes, has 57 people to the square mile, Africa 12, and South America 7. The only countries that have a population which is nearly as thin as that of Australia are Asiatic Russia with 3·7 and Arabia, which has been estimated to have 2 per square mile. Outside the Polar regions the only extensive countries with so sparse a population are parts of South Africa and the French Sahara. Canada has a population of 1·9 per square mile and Newfoundland and Labrador a population of 1·49 per square mile.

Nevertheless in spite of its comparative emptiness Australia has done well during the last half century in the increase of its population. Canada, in spite of the great advantages of proximity to the United States and easy access from Europe has taken two and a half centuries to attain its population, including aborigines, of a little over 7,000,000. The Australian population has practically all entered since the discovery of the gold-fields in 1851. The original settlement in Sydney consisted of about 1035 persons. In 1800 the white population of Australia was a little over 5000. In 1820 it was 33,000; in 1830 it was 70,000; by 1840, owing to the developing pastoral industries, it had grown to 190,000; but in 1851, the year of the discovery of the first important gold-fields, the population ran up to 437,665.

At the end of the first sixty years of its colonisation the white population of Australia numbered only 405,000. Considering then its remote position and arid interior, Australia has done remarkably well to have gained an increase of 4,000,000 persons and to have multiplied its population elevenfold during the second sixty years of its history.

As so considerable a proportion of its population has come by immigration, the number of males in Australia is exceptionally high, there are 2,313,035 males as compared with 2,141,970 females. The proportion of males to females is higher than in any other important country, except New Zealand.

The great bulk of the Australian people belong to the European races. According to the census of 1911, the total number of persons derived from non-European races in the Commonwealth, excluding the aborigines but including half-castes, was 52,000, or 11¾ per cent., of whom the great majority, 38,690, were Asiatics. The largest number of non-European inhabitants is in New South Wales; but the highest proportion is in Queensland and Westralia, in each of which about a quarter of the population is Asiatic.

The number of aborigines is roughly estimated at

about 100,000, but as most of them live in the remote parts of northern and north-western Australia no exact figures are available. Their number was probably always small.

According to the census of 1901, 77 per cent. of the population belonging to the European race were born in Australia, 18 per cent. in the British Isles, 1 per cent. in Germany, 1·25 per cent. in Asia. For the Commonwealth as a whole 98 per cent. of the population has been born either in Australia or in Europe.

In spite of its proximity to the teeming populations of Asia the number of Asiatic inhabitants in Australia is still low, a result largely due to the measures taken to prevent the country being swamped with Asiatics. They were entering the country in 1886 in such a rapidly increasing stream that drastic legislation was passed to prevent Australia suffering the fate of Hawaii and having its labour completely orientalized.

CHAPTER II

GENERAL DESCRIPTION OF AUSTRALIA

The Commonwealth of Australia consists of the continent of Australia, the large island of Tasmania, and numerous smaller islands. Its area is 2,974,581 square miles, or about three quarters that of Europe, a third of North America, a quarter of Africa, or about a sixth of Asia. The mainland is compact in form; it is somewhat kidney-shaped, the greatest length lying nearly along the Tropic of Capricorn; and no less than 1,149,320 square miles or more than a third of the whole Commonwealth lies within the tropics. Northern Australia is separated by Torres Strait and the Arafura Sea from the islands of the Malay Archipelago, with which Australia had its last land connection, when, as its name implies, it was the austral (Lat. *australis* = southern) part of Asia. On the remaining sides Australia has long been separated from other lands; though it once extended westward into the Indian Ocean, eastward into the South Pacific, and at an earlier time southward into the Southern Ocean.

The long isolation of Australia is the factor which has governed its political and physical geography.

It was probably the last habitable continent to be reached by man; and it was the last discovered and colonised from Europe. Australia has never exercised in Europe the sentimental attraction of Africa; and it is cut off from that close personal intercourse with the British Isles which is possible in Canada to all classes of the community. Australia has in consequence remained less known and has been more seriously misunderstood than any of the other white colonies of the Empire.

Australia still suffers from the misleading idea that the continent consists of a narrow ring of fertile land around a vast internal desert. This conception is so greatly exaggerated that it amounts to a geographical caricature. The term desert is indefinite. It is used in the Bible for a waste place which is uninhabited, but not necessarily uninhabitable; and Sir Walter Scott and R. L. Stevenson adopted it in the same sense when they described as deserts the rain-sodden Grampians and the back country of New England with its labyrinth of lakes and swamps. The word has however gradually acquired in geography a more restricted meaning; it is applied to land which is not occupied or but thinly occupied owing to the arid nature of the climate. As Prof. Walther, a leading authority on the subject, has truly remarked no rigid boundary line can be drawn between desert and not desert.

Nevertheless it has been proposed to define as desert all areas having an average annual rainfall of less than ten inches. It has been pointed out by Goodchild that an average is unsatisfactory, since occasional thunderstorms, separated by long rainless intervals, might yield a fall of over ten inches a year and yet leave the country under desert conditions; so he regards the essential characteristic of the desert as a quantity, much below the average, of aqueous vapour in the air.

A large part of central Australia has such an arid climate that according to this definition it might not unjustly be described as desert; and the country around Lake Eyre, where the average rainfall is below five inches a year, represents extreme desert conditions.

With increasing knowledge of the interior of Australia the proportion known to have an annual rainfall of more than ten inches has steadily grown. No adequate rainfall records are yet available for many districts. Observations continued over many years are required for a reliable average; but large tracts that have been described as desert have a vegetation which could only have grown with a rainfall of over ten inches. The pioneers in the interior of western Australia were harassed by want of water, and some of them represented the country as a vast desert of spinifex and sand; but abundant

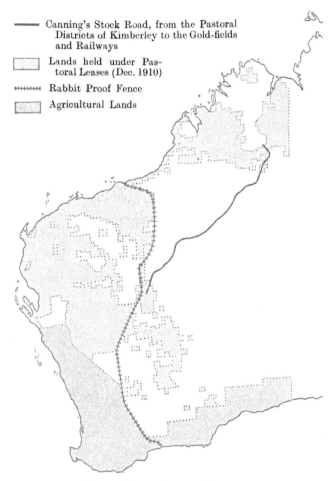

Fig. 2. The settlement of Westralia

water has been found in regions which were formerly regarded as waterless wastes. In fact, as shown by the sketch map Fig. 2, pastoral settlement has already extended over most of the western half of Westralia. The rich cattle breeding country of the northern part of that State has been reached by an overland road, which is watered by wells at intervals of from fifteen to twenty miles, and it crosses country which a previous generation of travellers believed to be passable only, and then with great difficulty, by well-organized caravans of camels.

The conception of the desert interior of Australia is however, true in part; for as most of the rain which falls on the land comes from the sea the rainfall is naturally greatest on the margins of the continents. Owing to its peninsular structure Europe (exclusive of Russia) has a rainfall unusually even in distribution; but all the other continents include tracts of internal desert. Australia is no exception to the rule that the rainfall is heaviest on the coast lands and diminishes steadily inland. Thus at Portland on the coast of Victoria the rainfall is 33 inches a year; but forty miles inland at Hamilton the average rainfall has diminished to $26\frac{3}{4}$ inches; while at Nhill, 100 miles further in, it has fallen to 17 inches; and 300 miles inland at Mildura it is under 11 inches.

The highest known rainfall is on the coast of Queensland at Innisfail (a town till recently known

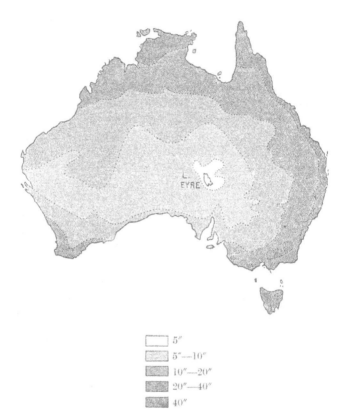

	5″
	5″—10″
	10″—20″
	20″—40″
	40″

Fig. 3. Rainfall Map of Australia

as Geraldton), where the average for the twenty-
five years, 1886 to 1910, is 149½ inches. The amount
diminishes inland and on a line to the south-west it
falls to 40 inches at a distance of 85 miles, to 30
inches at 120 miles, and to 20 inches at 200 miles.

The distribution of the zones of rainfall in
Australia is however somewhat irregular; and the
contrast between the well-watered coastal belt and
the arid interior is not clearly shown on some parts
of the southern and western coasts. The rainfall is
heaviest along the eastern coast, which is washed by
warm currents from the tropical seas. The winds
blowing inland on the eastern coasts of Australia
are warm and saturated with moisture. On reaching
the land they are forced to rise on to the eastern
highlands, where the mean temperature is lower than
that of the sea. Hence these currents of moist air
are cooled and drop their water in abundant rains.
The southern and western coasts of Australia are
influenced by cold currents coming from the Southern
Ocean; the winds which blow ashore are cool, and
during most of the year they become warmer as
they cross the land. These districts of Australia
therefore receive most of their rain in the winter.

The south-western corner of Australia includes
some high land, which secures a good rainfall for
that district; but when the winds blow inland over
the comparatively low country to the north of the

Great Australian Bight, or along the northern part of the main western coast, their moisture is not cooled and condensed and the rainfall is low. The Northern Territory of Australia and the northern districts of Westralia have a heavy rainfall brought by the monsoons which blow from the Indian Ocean. The monsoonal winds travel far inland and thus give a better rainfall to the Northern Territory and the northern part of Westralia than was originally expected. Between the region watered by these monsoonal rains, which are chiefly derived from the Indian Ocean to the north-west, and the region with the winter rains derived from the south and south-west, is the belt of Australia with the minimum rainfall. It extends from the south-western part of Queensland and the north-western part of New South Wales across South Australia and the southern interior of Westralia.

The development of Australia has been governed more directly than any other continent by its rainfall. Eastern Australia, owing to its better rainfall, has politically outstripped western Australia. The first successful colonies were New South Wales and Victoria, and later those of Tasmania and Queensland. The population of South Australia has remained comparatively small; and nearly the whole of that of Westralia, except on the mining fields, is concentrated in the south-western corner in the area of the heaviest rains.

CHAPTER III

THE PHYSICAL GEOGRAPHY OF AUSTRALIA

The unequal distribution of the rainfall in Australia is one result of the geographical unity of the continent. Australia owes its compact form to its unity of structure. All the other continents include areas which originally belonged to different continents, and the union of the once separated geographical units has been effected by the deposition of widespread sheets of sediments which now form the most fertile parts of the whole continent. Hence inland seas and great river valleys usually give easy access to the plains, which in most continents connect the old highland masses. All Australia belonged to the ancient continent of Gondwanaland, and though since its date the sea has twice penetrated far into Australia—in the Chalk Period going southward from the northern coast to Lake Eyre, and in later times extending northward from the Great Australian Bight and up the basin of the Murray— yet Australia has probably been one continuous land longer than any other continent. These ancient marine invasions have left wide plains which are covered by the most extensive areas of fertile soils in Australia; but as they have less than 20 inches rainfall and parts even less than 10 inches, they are mainly used for pastoral purposes, though the districts with a rainfall of 14 inches or even less are being now used for agriculture.

The greater rainfall near the sea has occasioned the striking differences between the coastlands and the interior, on which is founded the expression that Australia is a frame without a picture. This saying exaggerates both the sharpness and extent of this contrast, for several factors tend to establish a gradual passage from the fertile to the arid types of country. As the greater extension of Australia is west and east the whole country has a greater uniformity in climate than it would have if its main length were north and south. All the northern part is in the tropical zone while the rest is in the warm temperate zone. The prevalent winds and wind systems travel from west to east; they therefore cross the full length of the continent, and though the uplift of the winds on to the western plateau gives its western margin a fair rainfall, the elevation is not sufficient to collect all its moisture. Thus the distribution of the rain is more widely spread than in lands where the west winds have to pass at once over high mountains.

The contrast between the more arid western and the better watered eastern districts is explained by the nature of the mountains. Australia as a whole is a great plateau land. It is a fragment of a larger continent, the rest of which has been snapped off along great fractures. The land extended further in all directions, and its former extensions have foundered beneath the sea. The recent truncation of the country is well shown on both the eastern and western coasts, which are bordered by high plateaus. On the northern and southern coasts the ascent to the plateau is more gradual. Whereas it took years of search to find a practicable route from the eastern coast on to the eastern plateau, wide valleys and extensive lowlands run far inland, both northward from the Southern Ocean and southward from the seas of the Malay Archipelago. But even on the northern and southern coasts the chief railways are handicapped by having to begin their route inland by a long climb on to the plateau.

The mountain system of Australia is not determined by any dominant lines of folding of the earth's crust, like those which have formed the Alps and the Himalayas. Australia was folded at an early period in the earth's history; and all its ancient fold-mountains have been long since worn down. The chief existing features in the relief of Australia are due to vertical earth-movements, by which some parts of the area have been raised into high plateaus, and others have sagged downward into deep basins.

The margins of the plateaus have been carved into valleys, which vary in character with the local rainfall and strength of the rivers. The eastern margin of the old plateau has been dissected by powerful streams into deep valleys, which are separated by steep sided and flat topped ridges; and in some districts river erosion has been so active that very little of the original surface has been left. The former existence of the plateau can however be recognized from several features in the topography; thus the neighbouring ridges all reach about the same height; there are no peaks rising boldly above the general level; and patches of gravels on the ridge-tops are remnants of the beds of rivers which once meandered over the old highland surface.

Western Australia on the other hand, owing to its smaller rainfall and feebler rivers, retains more of the old plateau surface. The valleys and gullies which have notched the edge of the plateau are shallower, and less numerous, than they are around the Eastern Highlands; and the inner part of the plateau is a vast gently undulating country, with low rounded hills, except where some hard wind-etched boss of rock, rises abruptly from the plains. Wide shallow depressions run together like the converging branches of a river; and these valleys are divided by the irregularities of their floors into basins, which in wet seasons may contain lakes of little depth; but usually they are sheets of salt incrusted clay, or damp mud and salt marsh. These are the lakes which are the most conspicuous feature in the maps of Westralia and are the remains of the old river system which discharged to the Southern Ocean, when the level of the country was about 800 feet lower than it is now.

Owing to the absence of recent fold mountains the relief of the continent depends on the weathering of the old plateau, and the formation of highlands and lowlands by the uplift or subsidence of wide tracts of country.

Australia has been divided into three divisions by the subsidence of a belt which extends across the continent from the Gulf of Carpentaria to the plains beside the lower part of the Murray River. These three divisions are the East Australian Highlands, the Central Plains and the Western Plateau.

The East Australian Highlands. The East Australian Highlands consist of the belt of mountainous country which extends from Cape York Peninsula in northern Queensland to Victoria and is continued beyond Bass Strait by the island block of Tasmania. These highlands include the most characteristic of Australian mountains. They are essentially a great plateau, which has either been raised in recent geological times, or has been left upraised owing to the sinking of the land on both sides of it. The

plateau height varies usually from about 1000 to
2000 feet, but with wide areas between 2000 and

------- 1000 ft contour

▢ Area 1000 ft or more above sea level

Fig. 4. The Physical Divisions of Australia

3000 feet in New South Wales. It rises on Mount
Kosciusko to 7256 feet, the highest ground in
Australia and falls as low as 2000 feet on some of

the wide gaps or geocols, as Taylor has called them, which break across it. On the eastern or Pacific side it has a steep face, owing to the land having sunk along great folds or fractures. Rivers and streams have eaten their way backward into the plateau, so that its eastern side is the most rugged land in Australia. For years the eastern face of the Highlands to the west of Sydney proved insurmountable; and no access inland could be found from Brisbane, till the botanist Allan Cunningham found a way through Cunningham Gap from the forest-clad valley near Brisbane to the open plains of the Darling Downs. He thus discovered the most fertile and easily developed land in Queensland.

The western slope of the East Australian Highlands is usually long and falls more gradually, so that the main drainage from the Highlands is westward into the interior and discharges through the Murray to the southern coast. The eastern drainage is through many short and often torrential rivers to the Pacific.

The East Australian Highlands consist of four main plateaus; on the north is that of north-eastern Queensland extending behind the coast from Cooktown for 300 miles southward to Townsville. It includes the Bellenden Ker Mountains (5440 feet) and the Charters Towers Goldfield and is bounded to the south by the basin of the Belyando River (the

southern branch of the Burdekin River). The land
rises again to the plateau of the Carnarvon Range.
This ends to the south at the gap between the heads
of the Dawson River, which flows to the sea past
Rockhampton, and the Condamine River, an upper
tributary of the Darling.

The third plateau extends from the high ground
around Toowoomba, to the west of Brisbane, southward into New South Wales; it includes south-
eastern Queensland and the New England Plateau
of New South Wales; this plateau has an area of
about 5000 square miles, most of which is over 3000
feet above sea level. The contrast between the
irregular country along the eastern margin of this
plateau and its level top may be realized from the
course of the railway from Sydney northward to
Brisbane. Instead of following the coast, the line
is carried inland on to the plateau and rises at Ben
Lomond to 5000 feet above sea level, and passes
close to the highest summit on the New England
Plateau; for the easiest route was along the water-
shed as it thus avoided both the intensely broken
canyon-reft country to the east, and many deep
valleys which drain westward to the Darling. The
New England Plateau ends abruptly to the south
with the lowland of the Hunter Valley, which is
occupied by the coal field of New South Wales.
This great break across the Highlands is called by

Taylor the Cassilis geocol, from the town at its head.
The term indicates the great width of the pass or col.

South of this gap is the fourth plateau, the Blue
Mountains which rise to the west of Sydney to the
height of from 2000 to 4000 feet above sea level.
Some of its features were described by Darwin.
David has shown that the eastern face is due to a
great earth-fold, by which the former eastern continuation of the Blue Mountain plateau has sunk,
so that it forms the lowlands around Sydney, and
still further east has foundered beneath the sea.
Andrews, Süssmilch, and Taylor have shown that the
East Highlands in New South Wales are due to
earth movements of very recent age and to great
fractures as well as to folding.

The fifth of the chief eastern plateaus is the
Monaro Tableland which is separated from the Blue
Mountains by the depression, on the floor of which
lies the basin of Lake George; south of this lake the
level rises to the great Monaro Tableland, which is
the highest area of the East Australian Highlands,
and rises on Mount Kosciusko to 7256 feet. This
Monaro Tableland extends westward into Victoria
and its extension forms the Victoria Highlands;
while further south, isolated by Bass Strait, its
former continuation exists as the rugged island block
of Tasmania.

The East Australian Highlands are in places

separated from the sea by tracts of low coast land.
Some of these coast plains occur where soft rocks
have been worn away by rivers; but the most
extensive are depressions due to the sinking of blocks
of the earth's crust. Thus Sydney is in an area
which is bounded on all sides except seaward by
high plateaus; the Sydney basin is a sunkland.
Lake George lies in another; the upper valley of the
Murrumbidgee according to Griffith Taylor and Süssmilch is a rift valley, for it has been formed by the
sinking of a comparatively narrow strip of land
between two long parallel fractures. Numerous
smaller sunklands occur in the Victorian and Queensland Highlands. The coast of Queensland has also
sunk, and a deeper parallel subsidence to the east
doubtless marks the long line of the Great Barrier
Reef.

Central Plains. In striking contrast to the
abrupt descent of the Eastern Highlands to the
Pacific is their long gradual slope westward to the
great plains which extend from the Gulf of Carpentaria southward to the Murray. The floor of these
plains consists mainly of a sheet of clays which were
deposited in a sea that existed somewhat earlier than
the formation of our British Chalk. They include
on the north the basin of the Flinders River, which
issues in the Gulf of Carpentaria. Down their
southward slope the Diamantina River and Cooper

Creek flow, whenever they happen to contain any water, to Lake Eyre. This lake has no outlet and rests forty feet below sea level. To the south of this area the level rises to a low divide which separates the Lake Eyre basin from that of the Murray and its long tributary the Darling. The Murray River discharges to the Southern Ocean through a shallow outlet at the mouth of the great lagoon of Lake Alexandrina.

These Central Plains have as a whole an arid climate, and even those with a fair average rainfall are apt to be stricken by prolonged drought. They contain however the largest areas of good pastoral country in Australia; and they include in the Riverina and along the Lower Murray the wide wheat fields of southern New South Wales and of north-western Victoria, and also the productive irrigation settlements of Mildura and Renmark.

The northern and central parts of the Central Plains are partially watered by deep flowing wells. Bore holes through the clays beneath the plains reach sheets of sandstone saturated with water which is under such high pressure that it rises in the bore holes and overflows at the surface. This water is often too alkaline and insufficient in quantity for extensive use in irrigation; but it is of incalculable value for watering stock, for maintaining cattle routes, and for domestic use. Most of the water is probably an old accumulation, which has slowly collected from three different sources—water included in the beds at the time of their deposition, water which has drained into them from rainfall, and deep-seated or plutonic water which has risen from the interior of the earth, owing to the high temperature and the pressure of its included gases. This last source plays an important part in forcing the water to the surface.

Unfortunately this store of water is not inexhaustible. Many of the wells flow only for a few years and in most parts of the area watered by them the discharge has already fallen greatly. The pressure of the rising water has been reduced on an average one-third in the last five years; but after the wells have ceased to discharge automatically, they will doubtless yield by pumping a supply for a much longer period.

The Western Plateau. The third main division of Australia consists of the great Western Plateau, which is composed chiefly of very ancient rocks. It rises to the west of the Central Plains, and most of it varies in level from about 1000 to 2000 feet. Its surface is usually level or gently undulating; occasional blocks of hard rock form isolated table-lands, and tent-shaped and conical hills; and these are gradually reduced to bold rock pyramids or pillars. Some bands of old folded rocks form long

mountain ranges, such as the Macdonnell Ranges
near the centre of the continent and other ranges
in the Kimberley District of northern Westralia.
Most of the surface consists of undulating down-
like country and on the floors of the depressions are
wide level clay pans, which after rain form wastes
of mud or are covered by shallow sheets of salt
water. These "lakes" lie along the valleys of an
ancient river system, and as the land underwent
desiccation the rivers dwindled, until they could no
longer keep open their channels; banks of wind
drifted sand formed barriers across the valleys,
which were thus divided into detached lake basins,
and with the further drying up of the country, the
lake waters evaporated and left the lakes as sheets
of mud or clay. The gradual fall in the successive
levels in the chain of lakes enables the old river
system to be determined.

Owing to its position the Western Plateau receives
much less rain than the East Australian Highlands,
and much of the country was regarded as useless
desert. The first attempts to explore the interior
were foiled by the scarcity of water. Upon the discovery of the gold mines at Coolgardie the supply of
water was so precarious that the Government refused
to proclaim the settlement as a township; the whole
population indeed had once to retire until fresh
rains had refilled the pools and restarted the flow

into the soaks or shallow holes dug in the sand along
lines of drainage.   The gold-fields at Kalgoorlie could
not have reached their present development had not
the Westralian Government, by one of the most
daring of modern water supply undertakings, collected freshwater in a reservoir near the coast, and
thence pumped it over 350 miles inland, on the way
lifting it on to the plateau, to the height of 1500 feet.

At first all the interior of Westralia was regarded
as a waterless waste; but with longer experience of
the rains, and underground supplies, it is clear that
the country has far more rain and more water than
had been thought.   Areas that had been regarded as
a waste of sand and spinifex (the sharp spine-leaved
dune plant) have been found to be fair cattle country;
Canning's road, with its long line of good wells fifteen
to twenty miles apart, now provides an easy cattle
route, and mobs of cattle are driven along it for a
distance of about 1000 miles from the fertile downs
of Kimberley south-westward to the mining fields
(Fig. 2, p. 18).

The area believed to have a rainfall of less than
ten inches has already been considerably reduced,
and the recent official meteorological maps of
Australia show that it is still contracting. Canning's
road is useable as it traverses country consisting of
wide areas of sandstones, which store up the rainfall
and yield it in shallow wells.   But these sheets of

sandstone conceal the underlying gold-bearing rocks, so there is very little hope of gold mining in these districts of Westralia. Where the older rocks are exposed on the surface of the plateau, they contain quartz-lodes, some of which are rich in gold. The present prosperity of Westralia is due to the development of its gold mines, which, in the Golden Mile near Kalgoorlie, include the richest square mile known in mining history. Owing to the difficulty of access to these mines, the scarcity of water, the necessarily high cost of labour, and the complex and refractory nature of the ores, the working of these mines has been attended with unusual hindrances; it is only by reason of the remarkable skill and originality of the Australian miners that the gold mines have proved so profitable.

In the neighbourhood of the chief gold-fields the Western Plateau has a smooth level surface. This high plain is bounded to the west by a steep scarp, the Darling Range, where the existence of the numerous valleys that have been cut backward from this face have given the plateau an irregular surface. The Darling Range has been formed by the sinking of the land to the west. A belt of coastal plain extends from the foot of the Darling Range to the shore; this plain consists of very varied rocks which slope westward, and yield large quantities of water from deep wells.

The coastal belt and the western margin of the Western Plateau have a good rainfall and are occupied by forests of jarrah and karri, which yield the most valuable of Australian timber; and on the surface of the plateau as far inland as the good rains extend, is the agricultural area of southern Westralia. Northern Westralia is well watered by monsoonal rains from the Indian Ocean, and it contains much valuable pastoral and agricultural land, and some mining fields.

The Northern Territory also belongs to the Western Plateau. The southern part of this territory consists of arid plains, which are continuous with those of central Westralia; but to the north the level sinks gradually; the rains become heavier, and the country would naturally be expected to prove of high agricultural value. Mr Griffith Taylor, the physiographer to the Australian Meteorological Service, however remarks that "it does not appear to be very good cattle country, and though the rainfall is very heavy in summer, the soil is poor in plant food and the vegetation, on the whole, is scanty, except along the rivers." (*Federal Handbook to Australia*, 1914, p. 113.)

On the south, the great Western Plateau gradually descends in level to less than 1000 feet, and its old rocks pass below wide sheets of limestone, which were laid down at a time (the Miocene), when the Great

Australian Bight extended further inland, and the level of southern Australia was 800 or 1000 feet lower than it is now.

The south-eastern corner of the Western Plateau consists of the Highlands of South Australia, which are formed of rocks allied to those of the Macdonnell Ranges in central Australia and to the ranges of the Kimberley District of Westralia. The South Australian Highlands are now cut off from the main part of the Western Plateau by the Great Valley of South Australia, a rift valley which forms the basin of Lake Torrens and the long, drowned valley of Spencer Gulf. The South Australian Highlands face the Great Valley of South Australia in a bold steep scarp but descend more gradually eastward to the Murray plains.

Rivers. The rivers of Australia play a smaller part in its development than those of any other inhabited continent. The greatest river system is that of the Murray, which is a compound river formed by the junction of several once independent rivers, the Darling, Lachlan, Murrumbidgee and Hume or Upper Murray. These rivers drain the western slopes of the Eastern Highlands of New South Wales and southern Queensland, and the northern slopes of the Victorian Highlands. The river judged by length is one of the great rivers of the world, for its length from the sea to the most distant sources of the Darling is 3280 miles; but it undergoes such great changes of volume that its navigation is uncertain. The discharge from its mouth has occasionally even ceased altogether.

The other chief rivers of Australia, include the numerous short rivers that drain the eastern slope of the East Australian Highlands, the Snowy River and the Yarra which flow through Victoria to the Southern Ocean, the Swan River in Westralia, and the Roper and Victoria Rivers of the Northern Territory.

CHAPTER IV

RELATIONS OF THE FAUNA AND FLORA OF AUSTRALIA

Many Australian landscapes have a strong general resemblance to English scenery. There are wide areas of rolling grass covered downs, with here and there gnarled trees like wind-bent oaks or clumps looking like white trunked birches, and beside the streams are trees with the drooping foliage of the weeping willow. The similarity is increased by the animals; many of the birds so resemble our own that they are known as magpies, tits, larks, jays and wrens; in these cases the resemblances are superficial; but there are hawks, owls, falcons, crows, herons, swallows, pigeons, teal, duck, kingfishers and many other birds closely related to those of Europe. Hiding in the reeds or burrowing in the sandhills are native mammals called rats and hares. Closer examination shows that the resemblances are frequently due to different organisms having acquired similar forms in obedience to the same mechanical conditions; and a first ramble in the Australian bush leaves, on a British naturalist, a deep impression of the fundamental differences between the faunas and floras of Australia and Europe. The weeping willow proves to be a gum, the oak-like trees to be acacias; the magpie is a shrike, and the so-called rats, moles and hares are pouched mammals. Subsequent excursions will disclose the presence of a considerable proportion of Australian mammals allied to the rodents and bats of Eurasia and of abundance of plants similar to the European, such as our common bracken, and forests of true beech (*Fagus*).

Nevertheless more intimate acquaintance with the country deepens the impression of the distinctive character of the Australian animals and plants. The characteristic mammals are marsupials, such as kangaroos, wallabies and bandicoots, or are egg-laying monotremes like the duckbill; the rivers contain some archaic fish, and the sea some shell-fish which disappeared from Europe in a far distant geological time. The special features of the flora are the predominance of the eucalyptus and the absence of our common deciduous trees, such as the oak, elm and birch, and of all our fruit trees, although the climate is well suited for them.

The unique feature of Australian life shows that Australia has been isolated from the rest of the world by some insuperable barrier, and the familiar explanation is that Australia has been an island ever since mammals began to multiply upon the earth. Hence it is concluded that Australia was last connected by land with Asia during or at the end of the formation of the Chalk.

The geological evidence collected in recent years however, renders it improbable that the isolation of Australia was effected so early. The island chain which extends from the western side of the Malay Archipelago to New Guinea, including Sumatra, Java, Bali, Lombok, Sumbawa and Timor, consists of fragments of a mountain chain which was formed by the crumpling of a band of the earth's crust at about the same date as the formation of the Alps. The islands are all links of a chain which, in recent geological times (late Miocene to Pliocene) must have been continuous from Sumatra to the islands of western New Guinea and doubtless to New Guinea itself. This mountain chain was probably soon broken by cross fractures into a chain of islands; but their structure and arrangement are inexplicable except on the view that they once formed a continuous land.

The great puzzle of Australian biology is therefore why the Australian organisms did not cross to Asia and why the Asiatic did not work their way eastward to Australia. According to Wallace the Australian and Asiatic regions are separated by the strait between the islands of Bali and Lombok, where is placed the biological divide known as "Wallace's line." That line is however less definite than was supposed. The Australian and Asiatic elements overlap in the Malay Archipelago and are divided by a transitional zone instead of by a sharp line. The transitional zone is however surprisingly narrow, and the fact remains that none of the larger mammals of the other continents ever reached Australia.

The geological and biological evidence are therefore in apparent conflict. For geology provides a land bridge from Asia to Australia of which the plants and animals made no appreciable use. Two alternative explanations suggest themselves. It may be that the land connection consisted of a mountain chain, which was high and narrow, and had lofty branches to the north, while its lower flanks were covered by dense forest; the animals that could have crossed the mountains could not force their way through the jungles, so that there was no migration along this mountain land except of small animals such as rats and mice, of which a considerable number of forms reached Australia. That a mountain chain could have been continuous and yet have formed so complete a barrier to the migration of animals may appear improbable; and it may be that the Asiatic end of this land bridge was itself isolated by sea from the mainland of the old world, until after the Malaysian mountain band was broken up by cross fractures like that which formed the strait between Bali and Lombok and continued through Macassar Strait, between Borneo and Celebes. Hence the land line may have been severed before the larger mammals gained access to its western end. This suggestion may be set aside at any time by the discovery of fossil mammals of Miocene age, in the Malay Archipelago; and if so, the absence of the higher mammals from Australia must be owing to some hindrances to migration due to the geographical conditions of the land such as prevented the tiger reaching Borneo. It is clear that the Malay Archipelago was traversed in recent geological times by a mountain chain which united areas that are now biologically Asiatic to islands that are now biologically Australian.

CHAPTER V

THE ABORIGINAL INHABITANTS OF AUSTRALIA

An Australian native, according to accepted usage, is a member of the white race who has been born in Australia. The tribes which inhabited the country when it was colonised are known as black-fellows or aboriginals. Dampier, the first European to describe them, reported that they were "blinking creatures," with frizzled hair and "the most unpleasant Looks and the worst Features of any People that ever I saw, tho I have seen great variety of Savages." His unfavourable verdict appeared to be confirmed by the information collected by the early colonists. For they found that the aboriginals had no knowledge of metals, pottery, the bow and arrow, of weaving fabrics, or of cultivating the land; they had no domestic animals, except packs of dingoes. Their tools were of stone, bone, and wood; they made string by plaiting hair and various fibres; they fed only on the products of the chase, on caterpillars and other insects, and on scanty wild plant foods; they had no permanent houses or huts and were compelled continually to wander, as they exhausted the scanty local supplies of food. Beside the rivers and the coast, where fish and shell-fish were inexhaustible, they had more durable settlements, but even in these they trusted to bivouacs and the rudest of rough shelters. Fear of spirits prevented them occupying caves. The social customs of the people also appeared very primitive; and when it was discovered, that Australia is now inhabited by the most ancient existing types of back-boned animals which have survived there owing to isolation from the rest of the world, the belief became general that the Australian aborigines are the most primitive existing race of mankind. This conclusion has been advocated in recent years by Sir J. G. Frazer who holds (*Totemism and Exogamy* I, 1910, p. 342) that their material culture, beliefs and social customs indicate that the Australians are the lowest of all existing races of men about whom we possess accurate information. In accordance with this view it was hoped that the Australians retained the culture as well as the tools of the European stone age.

This claim and hope rested on a disputed interpretation of the social customs of the aborigines; and if to be lowest in the scale of humanity means the closest affinity to the ancestor of the human family, this conclusion seems improbable. The strongest argument advanced in its support was the asserted resemblance of the skeleton of the

Australian aboriginals to that of the Neanderthal race, which lived in Europe in the older stone age. This resemblance has been emphatically denied by so high an authority as Prof. Marcellin Boule. He admits that the Neanderthal and Australian skulls agree in length, in the strength of the teeth, the width of the nose and the depth of the notch above the nose. But he says the differences are more numerous and fundamental. "They leap to the eyes and have no need of being demonstrated." So much importance has often been attached to the points common between the skulls that the following translation of Prof. Boule's comparison of the two races may be useful. "The Australian," he says, "is notably taller; his head is much less capacious; his cranium is more dolichocephalic—not platy-cephalic or often even scaphocephalic; its archi-tecture is in all respects that of the modern human cranium. The occipital region is not depressed, but only appears so. The face is very short, instead of being long; its feeble prognathism is almost ex-clusively subnasal. The malar bones are convex, the canine fossae are very much accentuated. The facial physiognomy due to these features is exactly the opposite of the physiognomy presented by the crania of La Chapelle-aux-Saints and of Gibraltar. The lower jaw which is relatively feeble, most often presents a projecting chin. The vertebral column is long and slender, instead of being short and thick. The bones of the arms are also very graceful; the forearm is long in proportion to the arm; each of these bones is distinguished from the same bone in the fossil skeletons by their characters being diametrically opposed." Prof. Boule concludes that the Australian type "has nothing in common with the type of Neanderthal, except a few localized features in the frontal and fronto-nasal regions."

The now extinct Tasmanians were closely allied to people who lived in New Guinea. The Tasmanians had scanty short woolly hair, thick lips and black skins; their culture was more primitive than that of the Australians, for their stone tools were made by chipping only, whereas the Australians made implements with ground edges. The Tasmanian tools therefore correspond in this respect to those of the older stone age (Palaeolithic) of Europe, whereas the ground-edged Australian tools correspond to those of the later stone age (Neolithic).

The origin of the Tasmanians and the manner of their entry into Tasmania are still uncertain. According to one theory the Tasmanians once occupied Australia and reached Tasmania when it was still joined to the mainland; and after the formation of Bass Strait they were exterminated in Australia by the arrival there of the present aborigines. This view cannot be regarded as

established until deposits containing stone tools
only of the Tasmanian type are found on the mainland. Some of the Tasmanian implements are of the
kind known as Mousterian, after those of one stage of
the earlier stone age of Europe; and though similar
chipped stones have been found in Australia they
have there been found in or above deposits containing stone tools of a much later type. No
evidence has yet been found in Australia of its
former occupation by the Tasmanian race[1].

The alternative theory is that the Tasmanians
travelled southward along the eastern coast of
Australia, over land which has now sunk beneath
the Pacific. Since the date.when Huxley made this
suggestion it has been proved that the present
coast line of Australia is of very recent formation
and has been determined by the subsidence of the
land to the east, so that his hypothesis is consistent
with subsequent geological discoveries.

If the Tasmanians entered Tasmania by land
they must have been there a very long time. The
land connection across Bass Strait, which existed
in the Pliocene Period, perhaps lasted later; but it
was broken before the Dingo reached south-eastern

[1] Some Tasmanian-Australian half-breeds who were found in
Victoria were probably due to Tasmanians landed on the mainland
by the sealers and whalers, who frequented the coasts before the
settlement of Victoria.

Australia and so long ago that the Wombat of Tasmania and some other of its marsupials have had time to change into species distinct from those on the mainland.

It is therefore possible that the Tasmanians after working their way southward along the eastern coast of Australia may have crossed Bass Strait from island to island on the rude reed-built canoes, in which Bonwick saw them put to sea in even rough weather.

The aborigines of Australia belong to a very different race from the Tasmanians. It is generally agreed that the races of mankind may be divided into three primary groups. The best known names for these groups are the Caucasian, Mongolian and Negro, which are those of leading sections in each group. The names are not satisfactory when used for the whole groups; but they are so well known that they are the most convenient terms available. The members of the Caucasian group have straight or wavy hair[1], and include all the white people and many races with dark or even black skins. The

[1] According to the hair the Australians belong to the division of mankind known as Leiotrichi (smooth-haired) and the Tasmanians to the other division, the Ulotrichi (curly-haired). The fundamental distinctness of the Australians and Tasmanians has been recently reaffirmed by Sir William Turner (Nov. 1914), who regards the latter as nearly related to the negritoes who live among the mountains of New Guinea.

Mongolian group is characterized by long lank black hair, and usually by high cheek bones and almond-shaped eyes; it includes the aboriginal inhabitants of America as well as most of the people of eastern Asia and a few European races such as the Hungarians and Lapps. The Negro group, which includes the tribes of New Guinea and some adjacent islands as well as the negro tribes of Africa, have short woolly hair, dark brown to black skins, projecting jaws, and thick lips.

According to this classification the Tasmanian and Australian aborigines belong to different primary divisions of mankind, for the Tasmanian is a negro and the Australian is a dark skinned Caucasian. The Australian belongs to a race known as the pre-Dravidian, of which remnants survive in India, Ceylon, and some of the islands of the Malay Archipelago. The Australian is not only a later arrival in Australasia than the people of New Guinea and Tasmania, but he belongs to a higher and more specialized race. His primitive-looking habits are probably adaptations to life on the arid plains of inner Australia. He doubtless entered Australia from the Malay Archipelago, and possibly as Sir George Grey suggested, on the north-western coast; and he may have arrived when the sea between the region of Timor and the opposite coast of Australia was narrower than it is at present. After landing

4—2

somewhere on the northern coast he would have
spread southward, becoming adapted during the
journey to a nomadic life on the plains. At what
date he first landed in Australia is unknown; but
the evidence that he is a recent arrival in south-
eastern Australia, though negative, is very weighty.

It is remarkable that Australia is the only inhabited continent which has not provided direct
proof of the antiquity of man, by the discovery
of his stone implements in ancient deposits. The
gravels of south-eastern Australia have been searched
by gold miners more thoroughly than those of any
other part of the world; yet no certain trace of
man has been found there in beds of any considerable age. Again, though many of the volcanoes of
Victoria must have been in eruption at most a few
thousand years ago, there is no reliable tradition that
any of them were ever seen in action by the aborigines.
Some supposed footprints at Warnambool, a cut
bone found under a lava flow near Ballarat, a stone
implement below the soil near Maryborough (Vic.)
and a kitchen midden beneath a few feet of silt and
associated with dugong bones at Shea's Creek near
Sydney, have each been advanced as possible
evidence of the antiquity of man in Australia; but
in each case the evidence is either untrustworthy or
may be relatively modern. The arguments advanced
by R. Etheridge for Queensland, and by Brough

Smyth and the author for Victoria to show that there is no geological evidence of the antiquity of the Australians, are still unshaken[1]. Mr Chapman of the National Museum, Melbourne, writing in 1914, reaffirms this conclusion. He says (*Australasian Fossils*, p. 303) "So far no human remains or handiwork in the form of chipped implements have been found in other than superficial deposits, either in Tasmania or Australia."

The claim that the Australian is an archaic race therefore rests on the interpretation of his customs and beliefs; and the view that the culture of the Australian aborigines is simple and primitive has been rejected by some authorities who regard it as compound and as containing several elements, some of which are comparatively modern. The primitive features are explained as due to his primitive conditions of life; a settled agricultural or pastoral life being impossible, the working of useful metals was impracticable, and warm clothes and substantial huts unnecessary. So the wandering Australian clans may have lost arts practised by their ancestors. They could only live in small scattered groups, as large communities could not be fed. Under such

[1] A skull which was found many years ago on the surface in a gulley at Talgai in Queensland and is now under investigation, may prove a greater antiquity for man in Australia than any other evidence yet discovered, and that in northern Australia he was contemporary with the extinct giant marsupials.

conditions speech naturally varied quickly, and the languages of the different clans became mutually unintelligible, though their common origin is shown by their grammar. Unintelligibility in speech would have increased the chance of intertribal quarrels and lessened intercourse, so that the people would more and more have become isolated packs of hunters, and inbreeding became the most serious danger to the race. This evil has however been lessened by the adoption of a marriage system based on "exogamy"; each group is divided into two, four, or more classes or castes, and marriage within the same class is prohibited. The members of one class may be allowed to marry only with one other class, the children are regarded as belonging to a third class and may only marry the member of a fourth. These marriage rules in some tribes became so complex and the marriage restrictions so numerous that they proved impracticable.

These marriage castes are usually named after some animal or plant which is the totem of the class; and the origin of these totemic groups is a very controverted question. According to Haddon, the totemic groups are clans which have been named after the animals or plants which were their chief food. Sir J. G. Frazer has suggested successively three distinct theories of their origin. According to his first theory the totem was some object in which the

external soul was deposited for safety. Subsequently
he explained the totems as connected with magic
rites which were instituted to supply the community
with food, and this theory was supported by Prof.
Spencer from Australian evidence. Frazer's last
hypothesis is that totemism is due to the primitive
attempt to explain childbirth, which is attributed
simply to a spirit having entered the mother from
some object in which it had taken refuge. But the
view that such intelligent naturalists as the Australian aborigines are ignorant of paternity is difficult
of belief; especially as it is opposed by direct evidence
from reliable early observers. Thus according to
Howitt, the aborigines said their marriage restrictions
were adopted to avoid mixing the blood. Hence the
totemic groups and the rites connected with them are
not necessarily archaic.

The religion of the aborigines is a form of fetichism.
It involves an intense belief in reincarnation and in
a closely surrounding spirit world whose inhabitants
have to be propitiated by magic rites in order to
secure their help or avert their wrath. These rites
are performed at ceremonies known as corrobories,
which are usually accompanied by elaborate dances.

The mental and moral characters of the Australian
aborigines have both been sadly maligned. It has
been stated that they are unable to think intelligently
or to count beyond a few simple numbers. But they

are expert naturalists; their skill as trackers is probably unequalled by any other race; they have proved first rate stockmen; and aboriginal children at the schools on the reserves have often shown themselves very apt pupils and above the average in intelligence.

They were naturally one of the gentlest, kindliest, and most honest of aboriginal people; it was only in northern Australia where they had suffered centuries of ill-treatment by Malays or when goaded by injustice that they became actively hostile to the Europeans. As a rule they quietly withdrew before the advance of settlement and even passively permitted the appropriation of their lands by the colonists.

Their numbers in Australia were probably always small; the total in Victoria, on the occupation of the colony in 1836, is estimated as having been only from 6000 to 8000; and though they were far more numerous in northern Australia the estimate that the total number was only about 150,000 is not improbable. In recent years they are said to have increased in some districts, where they have more regular food and tribal wars have been stopped. Nevertheless when forced to adopt fresh habits they fall easy victims to new diseases.

The reduction in their numbers has been attributed to systematic massacre by the whites. The aborigines are however now fewest in Victoria, where there are only 136 left, although there is no doubt that they were always most conscientiously protected there both by the Government and by the private settlers. For instance, in 1842, five years after the foundation of Melbourne, three settlers near Colac were accused of the murder of three aboriginal women. The men were tried in Melbourne; the evidence was apparently not conclusive and they were acquitted by the jury. The Judge in dismissing the men warned them, that had they been found guilty, no interest would have saved them from the gallows; and after this emphatic pronouncement that the lives of the aborigines would be held sacred by the Government, as McCombie remarked in his *History of Victoria* (1858, p. 90), the Victorian aborigines ran no risk of unprovoked murder.

No doubt, in the remoter regions of Australia, where the pioneers were widely scattered, the aborigines numerous and wild, murders occurred on both sides and those of the whites were mercilessly avenged; and in the local wars the fighting no doubt tended to degenerate into mere nigger-hunting. Nevertheless the reduction in the number of the aborigines has been due more to nature than to man.

The worst ill-treatment of the blacks in recent decades was in Westralia, after the colony was granted self-government; for distrustful of the colonists, the Imperial Government reserved the control of the blackfellows. The results were deplorable, and the arrangement was altered; and when the Westralian Government was made responsible for the care of its aboriginals the evils which had grown up under the previous system were promptly and energetically suppressed.

CHAPTER VI

THE PRODUCTS OF AUSTRALIA

The total wealth produced annually by Australia is about £206,000,000 or over £44 per head of the population, which is a greater total than that of any other country or continent. The foundation of this wealth was based on the production of raw materials of which only the minerals are native to Australia, for the pastoral and agricultural industries depend on the exotic sheep and cow, and on imported grains and grasses. The minerals were only discovered and developed after the country had been opened up by pastoralists.

Pastoral. The first industry that was greatly successful in Australia was that of sheep rearing for wool. Capt. Macarthur, one of the most turbulent officers of the Sydney garrison, realized how admirably the Australian climate was suited for the raising of high quality wool; and as a result directly or indirectly, of his efforts, Australia has become the greatest producer of merino wool. Some half-bred merinos from Cape Colony, the descendants of a flock which had passed from Spain to Holland during the Spanish occupation of the Netherlands, had been brought into New South Wales; but the pure merino was unobtainable, for Spain had a monopoly of these sheep, and their export was prohibited under pain of death. There have been many versions of the story as to how this regulation was broken; but all the credit is usually given to Macarthur. According to one story they were smuggled out of Spain by the wife of the Ambassador to Spain; according to another they were a present from the King of Spain to George III during the Peninsular War. It is however clear that the first pure Spanish merinos which were imported to Australia came from the royal farm at Windsor, and that they served as the foundation of the Australian flocks.

Large areas in Australia are exceptionally well-adapted for sheep farming owing to the dry warm climate, rich turf, and the excellent natural hay formed by the dried herbage; so the merinos multiplied fast.

The search for fresh pastures for the growing flocks was the first motive for the exploration of the interior and the rich turf clad plains of Victoria were quickly occupied for sheep runs after Mitchell's discovery of their value.

By 1850 Australia owned 16,000,000 sheep; by 1860 the number had grown to 20,135,286; by 1890 it had increased to 97,881,221. Droughts, aided to some extent by the conversion of sheep runs to dairy farms, led to the fall of the number to less than 54,000,000 at the end of 1902; over 18,000,000 sheep had died that year; but the numbers had nearly recovered by 1911[1], when the total was 93,003,521 distributed as follows:

New South Wales	44,722,523
Queensland	20,740,981
Victoria	13,857,804
South Australia	6,171,907
Westralia	5,411,542
Tasmania	1,823,017
Northern Territory ...	50,983
Federal Capital Territory ...	224,764

Australia has therefore more sheep than any other country; the Argentine Republic ranks second with 67,000,000 (1908) and the Russian Empire third with nearly 63,000,000 (1910). The British Isles come fifth with, considering their size and the small areas available for sheep, the large number of about 30,500,000.

[1] In 1912 owing to drought the number fell to 83,000,000.

The wool production of Australia in 1911 is estimated at over 768,000,000 lbs., and the value of the wool exported, at over £26,000,000. The sheep were of value only for their wool and hides, until the

Fig. 5. Sheep-shearing by machinery in Queensland

discovery how to prepare tallow by boiling down the carcase; but in recent years the export of frozen meat, the value of which in 1910 was £2,161,622, has led to a change in the sheep, as they are no longer bred for wool alone. The skill of the Australian sheep breeder is perhaps unsurpassed. Owing to the size of the flocks the owners can afford to import high priced rams; and thus Australian wool has maintained a high standard. Varieties of wool required for some special purpose or to satisfy a freak of fashion have been produced and eradicated when they were no longer wanted.

The cattle industry of Australia has been less important than sheep farming. The total number of cattle in the Commonwealth in 1911 was nearly 12,000,000, or slightly less than the number in the United Kingdom. The chief cattle runs are in the interior and especially in western Queensland. The herds are driven to the ports or to the railways. Nearer the coast the cattle are mainly raised on dairy farms; and the development of the butter industry has led to a great increase in the number of dairy cattle. In 1911, the total production in the Commonwealth was over 211,000,000 lbs. of butter, nearly 16,000,000 lbs. of cheese and 23,000,000 lbs. of condensed and concentrated milk. The development of the butter trade did much to help Victoria to recover after the financial crisis of 1892.

Agriculture. Agriculture was necessarily the first industry attempted in Australia. By 1850 the quantity of land under cultivation was 198,000 acres in New South Wales, 52,190 acres in Victoria, and a total of 491,000 acres for the Commonwealth. In 1911–12 the total was 12,107,017 acres of which the chief crops are as follows:

	Acres	Value of Crop for 1911–12	
Wheat	7,427,804	£13,303,326	£1 15 10 per acre
Hay	2,518,288	10,288,960	3 11 9 ,,
Oats	616,857	1,463,780	2 7 6 ,,
Lucern and other Green Forage ...	424,440	1,217,000	2 17 4 ,,
Maize	340,065[1]	1,637,692	4 16 4 ,,
Sugar Cane ...	144,283[2]	—	—
Potatoes	130,463	2,296,797	17 12 1 ,,
Fruit	194,524	—	—
Vines	60,602	—	—

Wheat is the most important crop; and its great increase has been due to the spread of cultivation into arid areas and to the discovery that some Australian soils can be rendered productive by a small addition of phosphatic manure.

At one time it was thought that profitable wheat cultivation would be impossible where the rainfall fell below fourteen inches a year. The system of dry-farming, by which the land is so tilled as to economize the rainfall, has, however, extended wheat cultivation over areas such as the Ninety Mile Desert and Mallee districts of Victoria, which were once regarded as useless; and it is expected that wheat cultivation will be possible in Australia wherever

[1] Mainly in Queensland and New South Wales.
[2] Mainly in Queensland.

Fig. 6. Ploughing with the disc or "stump-jump plough." This plough is especially useful in cultivating forest land, which has not been thoroughly cleared of tree stumps

the soil is suitable and the annual rainfall is not less than ten inches.

The average yield of wheat throughout the Commonwealth in 1911 was 9·64 bushels per acre, which was unusually low owing to the unfavourable season; the highest average yield per acre in recent years was 13·73 bushels in 1909–10, and the average yield for the last ten years (1901–2 to 1911–12) was 10·48 bushels per acre. For comparison with these figures it may be noted that the average yield in 1910 was 30·48 bushels per acre in the United Kingdom; 29·29 bushels per acre in Germany; 15·42 bushels per acre in France; 13·70 bushels per acre in the United States and 9·75 bushels per acre in the Argentine.

The total value of the Australian wheat crop in 1911–12 was £13,303,396 or an average value per acre of £1. 15s. 10d.

Timber. Australia probably contains over 200,000,000 acres of known forest land and the forest reserves already proclaimed are one third the size of the United Kingdom. The trees are chiefly hard woods, some of which are very beautiful and some are so heavy that they sink in water; they are chiefly valuable owing to their strength and durability. These timbers are most useful for piles, girders, beams, sleepers, and wood paving; those most extensively worked are the jarrah and karri of Westralia, and the heavy ironbarks of the eastern

States. Most of the forests consist mainly of different species of Eucalyptus, which are popularly known as gums. Some of the trees are among the largest in

Fig. 7. Giant Gum Tree, South Australia

the world. Baron von Mueller, the distinguished
Australian botanist, accepted the height of some as
480 feet, but the latest official estimate accepts the
tallest as only 326 feet high, in which case they
would be a little shorter than the big trees of the
western United States.

Some Australian woods are known as "pines";
they grow especially in southern Queensland and
New South Wales; but Australia is poorly provided
with light woods which are suitable for most ordinary
purposes such as building construction, furniture and
for use in mines. Hence pine wood is purchased from
America, New Zealand, Scandinavia, Russia and
Japan and the Australian imports of timber are
greater than the exports; the value of undressed
timber imported in 1911 was £1,985,292, while that
exported was worth only £1,019,648.

For many years the forests were the great hin-
drance to the development of the country, for they
covered the most fertile land, which had to be
cleared by the slow process of killing the trees by
ring-barking—cutting a ring through the bark all
around the trunk—felling the trees, and ultimately
burning off the dead timber. It has often cost £30
to clear an acre. This process has been so energetically pursued in the accessible districts that alarm
has been felt at the widespread destruction of timber.
In recent years an agitation has been begun for the

preservation of the forests; . a state forestry school
has been established at Creswick in Victoria, and
government nurseries founded in each State in order
to discover the trees that are suitable for various
districts and to grow young trees with which to
replant districts where the destruction of the timber
has gone too far.   But Australia contains far more
forest than it can use, and as dairy land is more
profitable than forest, much more land will doubtless
be brought under cultivation by the apparently
wasteful policy of clearing.

Minerals.   The mineral resources of Australia are
of importance both from their direct contributions
to Australian wealth and indirectly from their
stimulus to the general development of the country.
The view has been expressed, by even so high an
authority as the late Sir Henry Wrixon, that the
Australian mining industry has been as a whole
unprofitable, the gold produced having cost more
than its value.   This estimate is doubtless correct
for some gold-fields, where mistakes and bad management have led to disastrous failures.   The magnificent profits from other fields have however more
than repaid the losses.   Gold mining began in
Victoria in 1851, and though it is the smallest of
the States on the mainland it has yielded gold to the
value of £295,000,000.   It is true that there have
been some expensive mining failures in Victoria, and

men have spent their lives in gold mining for a less reward than they might have gained in other callings; yet the industry in Victoria must have yielded on the whole a handsome profit. The idea that Victoria has during the past sixty years sunk on an average £5,000,000 per annum in gold mining is disproved by the statistics. Gold mining has in fact yielded Victoria a greater return than any other of her industries. The total value of the gold production has been greater than of the wool. Farming, sheep raising, and the timber industry have had their reverses; and abandoned runs, unprofitable farms, and commercial enterprises which have paid no dividend show that gold mining is not the only industry that is attended by costly failures.

The mineral wealth of Australia is colossal and varied; its most important yield has been gold, obtained from mines at Ballarat, Bendigo, and the many other gold-fields scattered through Victoria, from the East Highlands of New South Wales, from Mt Morgan, Charters Towers, Gympie and other fields in Queensland, and from Kalgoorlie with its "Golden Mile" and other rich gold-fields of Westralia.

South Australia has been least prolific in gold, and its fields, as at Tarcoola, are of secondary importance. The mines of Arltunga in the Northern Territory have been worked in spite of heavy costs, in the heart of the continent.

Among the other metal mines the most important have been those of silver and lead. The mines at Broken Hill in the far west of New South Wales proved so rich that they lowered the price of silver and lead throughout the world. The discovery of

Fig. 8. The Silver-Lead Mines of Broken Hill in the extreme west of New South Wales

copper mining in South Australia saved the young colony at the darkest period of its history; but in later times, the copper mines of New South Wales, notably at Cobar, those of Queensland and Mt Lyell in Tasmania, have been the chief producers. The tin mine of Mt Bischoff in north-western Tasmania is one of the world's great mines, but larger total yields of tin have been collected from the alluvial deposits on the plateau of northern New South Wales and the highlands of northern Queensland.

Fig. 9. The Mt Lyell Copper Mine, Western Tasmania

Good iron ores are known in all the States, but they have not hitherto been worked to any appreciable extent. Large iron-smelting works are now in process of erection, and ores near the shore of Spencer Gulf are being mined to supply them. Large accessible bodies of iron ore are available in Tasmania,

New South Wales, and Queensland, and smaller deposits are widely distributed.

Coal now ranks second among Australian minerals. The quantities of coal in eastern Australia are colossal; the coal field around Sydney and Newcastle in New South Wales is estimated to contain the largest quantity in any known single coal-field in the world. There are immense quantities of black coal in Queensland and of brown coal in Victoria.

The Australian coal is of such good quality, so cheaply mined, and so abundant, that Australia has no need to fear a coal famine, and should become one of the greatest producers of cheap power and iron.

In oil Australia is less well provided. There are large deposits of rich oil shale in New South Wales, but their working has not hitherto been commercially successful and the oil fields of New Guinea are still undeveloped.

The production of minerals in Australia to the end of 1911 has been as follows:

Gold	...	...	...	...	...	£536,196,981
Coal { Coal	...	£74,151,686 }				
{ Coke	...	1,976,214 }		...		78,415,961
{ Oil shale	...	2,288,061 }				
Silver and lead	...	...	...	...		65,849,880
Copper	...	...	...	...	...	59,149,716
Tin	...	...	...	...	...	30,227,626
Zinc, iron ore, antimony, gems, etc.				...		14,866,727
						£784,706,891

The relative proportions of the contributions from various industries to Australian wealth are estimated in the Commonwealth *Yearbook* (No. 7, p. 1053) for 1912, as follows:

Manufacturing	£57,022,000
Pastoral	51,615,000
Agriculture	45,754,000
Dairying, Poultry and Bee-farming ...	20,280,000
Mining	25,629,000
Forestry and Fisheries	6,432,000
	£206,732,000

CHAPTER VII

THE GOVERNMENT OF AUSTRALIA

The political development of Australia has many especially interesting and instructive features. The Australians have unique opportunities for political experiment and they are making full use of them. The conditions in the British Isles are so complex that it is difficult to trace the effects of any legislative change; it is therefore necessary to proceed with the utmost caution, since the overwhelming momentum of our institutions renders a reversal of policy almost impossible. But Australia is large enough for its experiments to be instructive, and sufficiently simple socially for their effects to be clearly recognizable.

Further, Australia has the advantage, if compared with South Africa and India, of being inhabited solely by a white race ; and if compared with Canada, Australia shows a greater predominance of the British race.

Australia is governed by two different types of governments—those of the States and of the Commonwealth. The Commonwealth includes the whole of Australia and Tasmania. It was founded in 1900 by the union of the six States, and it has since been entrusted with the direct administration of the Northern Territory. It is also responsible for the management of British New Guinea. The power of the Commonwealth Government is strictly limited to the functions enumerated in the constitution. It deals with questions which concern all the States; its chief departments deal with defence, foreign politics, customs and excise, postal and telegraph services, quarantine, currency, alien immigration and naturalisation, bankruptcy, patents, copyright, etc., and it can only interfere in industrial matters which affect more than one State. The Federal Government may acquire a railway by consent of the State in which it is situated. Thus the railway from Adelaide to Oodnadatta, which is intended to serve the Northern Territory and cross the Continent to Port Darwin, has been taken over by the Federal Government. It also is building the railway from Kalgoorlie to Port Augusta at the head of Spencer Gulf, which will unite the railways of Westralia with those of the south-eastern States.

The State Governments are responsible for railway development, education, police service, mining and industrial legislation, agriculture, fisheries and land settlement. Hence the most complex affairs are in the hands of the State Governments. It is often difficult to draw the line between the powers of the Commonwealth and of the States, for there is no easy rule which will determine when a subject affects the interests of two States sufficiently to bring it under the scope of the Commonwealth.

The establishment of the two sets of Governments is the result of the different requirements of Australia at different stages in its development. At first all the Australian settlements were governed from Sydney; but the colonies were far scattered and no attempt was made to occupy the intermediate coasts. It was not until other nations showed themselves desirous of possessing parts of Australia that the British Government annexed it all. By 1829 the British had formally taken possession of the whole of the continent through the occupation of Westralia and the establishment of the colony at Perth. These distant colonies could not all be satisfactorily governed from one centre, owing to the vastness of the distances between them, the

slowness of communication, and the varying needs
of the different districts. Tasmania, in 1825, was

Fig. 10.   The political subdivision of Australia.   In 1827 the
continent was subdivided into two colonies, New South Wales
and Westralia.   The former has since been divided into five
states, exclusive of the Federal Territory, around the future
capital of the Commonwealth.   Dotted lines mark temporary
boundaries

the first colony to be separated; Westralia was
started as an independent colony in 1829, and South

Australia in 1834–6. Victoria, which was at first known as the Port Phillip District of New South Wales, was established in 1834; its enterprising settlers soon demanded home rule. The Port Phillip District sent six representatives to the parliament in Sydney; but as a protest against the inconvenience of sending their members and referring their local questions to so distant a city, Melbourne, in 1848, elected Lord Grey as its member, and the Duke of Wellington, Lord Palmerston, Lord Brougham, Lord John Russell and Sir Robert Peel were nominated for the other seats. This protest no doubt helped the Home Government to realize the need for the subdivision of eastern Australia, and the Port Phillip District was separated in 1851 as the colony of Victoria. The colony of Queensland, previously known as the Moreton Bay District, was established in 1859. The land to the west of Queensland and north of South Australia remained part of New South Wales, which had however no direct contact with it, and in 1863 it was transferred to South Australia as the Northern Territory.

State Parliaments. Thus the continent is divided into six states; each has a Governor appointed by the Imperial Government, and each has a Parliament consisting of two chambers, the Legislative Council and the Legislative Assembly. The former is often referred to as the Upper and the latter as the Lower

House, though objection is taken to those terms. The Legislative Assembly is always elective and there is practically universal adult suffrage. Victoria was the last State to give women the vote; for it granted women's suffrage in 1900 probably to remove the anomaly, that while women, as electors for the Federal Parliament, had votes on naval and military matters, on foreign policy, interstate trade and customs, they had no votes on educational and social problems, or on local administration.

The members of the Legislative Assemblies receive an annual allowance, varying from £500 in New South Wales to £150 in Tasmania. The Assembly is elected for three years, but may be dissolved by the Governor.

The Legislative Councils are more varied in constitution than the Assemblies. The members of the Councils of New South Wales and Queensland are appointed for life by the Governor, but in the other States the Councillors are elected for six years on a franchise which is more limited than that for the Assembly and usually includes some property qualification. In New South Wales, Victoria and Queensland the members of the Council receive no salary.

The conflicts between the two houses of Parliament have occasioned the most serious trouble in the political history of Australia. These disputes have been especially determined in Victoria, where the upper house is elective and so can neither be dissolved nor swamped by the creation of new members. The first political deadlock due to a quarrel between the two chambers was over the adoption of protection. A strong majority of the Victorian Legislative Assembly was in favour of protection, while the majority of the Council was anxious to retain free trade. The Assembly regarded the question as purely financial and accordingly outside the proper sphere of the Council; it therefore, in 1865, joined the tariff to the bill formally passed each year to authorize the Government to collect the revenue. The Council could not amend this bill, but only pass or reject it. So it accepted the challenge and threw out the whole bill. The Government, supported by a majority of the Assembly, defied the Council, collected the revenue without legal authority, borrowed money from a bank, and allowed judgment to go by default when the bank sued for repayment. A general election of the Assembly reasserted the popular support of the Government, and the Council, though it again rejected the bill, ultimately passed it. The trouble was however not yet ended. The Governor, Sir Charles Darling, had supported the Government, and he was therefore recalled by the Colonial Office. The Assembly voted Sir Charles Darling its special thanks and his wife a grant of £20,000, but this grant the Council would not pass.

The new governor dismissed the former ministry and appointed another, whereupon the Assembly refused to vote supplies; and this deadlock lasted until the Colonial Office gave Darling a pension, whereupon Lady Darling declined the grant proposed to her.

A still more determined conflict between the two Victorian Chambers occurred in 1877. The Council rejected the annual Appropriation Bill, because regulations for the payment of members of the Assembly had been attached to it. As the Government had thus been refused the right to collect the revenue, it dismissed the police and Civil Service, retaining only a few men to act during the interval as caretakers of the public offices; and when the Council at length gave way, it had at the same time to accept a drastic measure for its own reform.

The influence of the Legislative Councils on Australian politics has been strongly anti-democratic. This resistance to change has at times been maintained with a sullen obstinacy, which prevented the development of a progressive conservative policy and secured the Labour party the support of many professional men who preferred the enterprising and generous ideals of Labour to the selfish fears of some of the champions of capital and privilege. The existing agitation by the Labour party to reduce the powers of the States, a change which might

ultimately prove prejudicial to the natural development of Australia, is apparently due to the habitual
opposition to reform by the State Legislative Councils.

The State Parliaments have initiated many important experiments, including the secret ballot at
elections, which was once known as the Australian
ballot. Another novelty which they have introduced to British constitutional government is the
referendum. It is adopted by the Commonwealth
in order to decide proposed alterations of the Constitution, or to allow the country to express a verdict
on a problem which neither political party wishes
to treat as a test question. In 1907 after a conflict
between its two State Houses, Queensland adopted
the referendum to settle such disputes. Preferential
voting is being tested in three of the States, having
been adopted by Tasmania in 1906 and by Victoria
and Westralia in 1911. The Tasmanian system is
the most complete and is based on Hare's principle
of a single transferable vote; but the experiments
have not been in operation for a sufficient time to
warrant any judgment upon their success.

Each State Government usually consists of a
Premier, a Treasurer, a Chief Secretary, an Attorney
General, and Ministers for the Departments of Lands,
Agriculture, Mines, Public Instruction, Railways,
Public Works, etc.; two or more departments may
share a Minister and all these offices do not exist in

all the States. The list of departments illustrates how many important duties are still left to the State Governments. Australia has been repeatedly criticized for maintaining fourteen houses of Parliament, for so small a population; but the choice of a Federal Constitution, like that of the United States of America, instead of a Union Government like that of South Africa, was deliberate and seems to have been the wisest.

Commonwealth Government. The central government was established to secure efficient services for defence and to look after external affairs and foreign trade. Such functions as the meteorological service and the lighting of the coasts were naturally also entrusted to the central government. But the different states are in such different stages of development, and vary so greatly in their local circumstances that the management of railways, roads, lands, schools and all ordinary local administration are left to the State Governments.

The State Parliaments with their local duties are as necessary in Australia as County Councils in England. If these local duties were managed for the western states from the eastern cities, the cost of administration would probably be increased; and if one department were established for the whole of Australia the local administration would have to be left to sub-offices in each state, and any gain might easily be more than neutralised by friction and waste of time and money.

The tendency in Australia has apparently always been towards very centralised government. The criticism is widely expressed in Australia that the Federal Departments are over-centralised. Sir Ian Hamilton, in his report on the Australian army, remarks that "the centralisation in the Defence Department at Melbourne exceeds anything I have experienced during more than forty years service in India, in the United Kingdom, and in every part of the world where troops administered by the British War Office are stationed." Similar opinions are expressed by members of the staff of other Federal Departments. This centralisation, though now perhaps carried to excess, was inevitable as the colonies became less isolated with the growth of railways and telegraphs, the spread of steam navigation, and the general improvement in internal communications. With the establishment of overland intercourse between the four eastern colonies, the inconveniences due to distance were lessened, but others were introduced owing to the separate policies of the colonies. Different fiscal systems gave no trouble when the settlements were separated by roadless wastes or by distances which rendered smuggling unprofitable; but as the settlers from the coast towns met in the interior, the adoption of free trade by New South Wales and of protection by Victoria led to difficulties. Moreover, as Australia became less isolated from Europe and Asia, as the Pacific problems began to trouble the political world, and as the people of south-eastern Asia ceased to stay at home, the States felt the need for closer association. The influences which had formerly divided Australia into separate colonies were now opposed by the need for union in several departments of government. Even during the establishment of the separate colonies the more farsighted of Australian statesmen had proposed the establishment of a "General Assembly of Delegates for all Australia." In 1891 a national Convention under the presidency of Sir Henry Parkes drafted a Federal Constitution; further conferences and conventions from 1895 to 1898 showed that the federal spirit was growing, and in 1899 the Commonwealth Act was passed and came into force on 1st January 1901.

This Act established a Federal Government and two Federal Chambers which are known as the Senate and the House of Representatives. The Federal Government includes a Governor General, who is also Commander-in-Chief and is appointed by the Imperial Government, a Federal High Court of Justice, two Houses of Parliament, and a Cabinet, which has usually consisted of eight members. The eight hold the nine offices of Premier, Treasurer,

Vice-President of the Executive Council, Attorney
General and Ministers for the Departments of Foreign
Affairs, Trade and Customs, Post Office, Defence and
Home Affairs.

The Constitution catalogues the respective duties
of the States and of the Commonwealth; but a
division by a mere list of subjects is impracticable,
for matters which concern more than one State are
necessarily the concern of the Federal Government.
Thus the regulation of industry is left to the States,
but any industrial conflict over the railways, shipping,
docks or carterage, might interrupt interstate communications and thus involve the Commonwealth.
The line between Federal and State authority is
incapable of precise definition, and already the
Federal Courts have dismissed as unconstitutional
various laws and regulations passed by the Federal
Parliament.

Thus the "New Protection" has been ruled out
as illegal.   Australian opinion is overwhelmingly in
favour of a protective commercial policy; but it is
also agreed that if a manufacturer be given the
advantage of a protective tariff, he must share the
benefit with his workmen by paying them fair wages,
and with the public by charging moderate prices for
his goods.   It was accordingly determined to exclude
from the advantages of the tariff any manufacturer
who endeavoured to secure an unfair share of them.

The method proposed was by excise duty and rebate.
For instance, if an import duty of say 5s. were
imposed on a pair of boots, then every boot-maker
in the Commonwealth would be charged an excise
tax of 5s. a pair on all he manufactured; and if he
paid his workmen fairly and sold his boots at a fair
price all the excise duty he had paid would be
returned to him as a rebate. This system imposed
a Federal tax to regulate the management of local
industries; and the Federal High Court has decided
that the Federal Government has under the Constitution no such powers of regulation. This excise
and rebate system would allow the Federal customs
to interfere in any branch of local administration;
and as the Labour party is in favour of extending
the central authority, it proposed referenda in 1911
and 1913 to amend the Constitution and transfer
to the Federal Government the control of trade,
commerce, trusts, trading corporations, the regulation of industrial employment and disputes, the
prevention and settlement of disputes on the State
railways, and the nationalisation of monopolies.
The proposals of the referendum of 1911 were less
comprehensive than those of 1913, but they were all
rejected by overwhelming majorities; the smallest
majority, that against the nationalisation of monopolies, was 736,392 to 488,668. At the referendum
of 1913, however, Queensland, Westralia, and South

Australia returned majorities for the proposed changes; in Victoria and Tasmania there were small majorities against them; and it was only the heavy majority against them in New South Wales that secured their rejection by a total of about 25,000 votes. As at the general election held simultaneously with the 1913 referendum the Labour Party was defeated, it appears probable that the proposed changes in the Constitution will some day be carried and the Federal authority made supreme in the industrial and commercial life of Australia.

The powers of the Federal High Court of Australia are limited to the matters that fall within the Federal sphere. Thus it has to decide on all questions of international law, foreign trade, customs, and conflicts between the States or residents in different States, or conflicts of interests that affect more than one State; and whether a question affects more than one State sufficiently to bring it under the Federal jurisdiction is obviously incapable of precise definition.

Commonwealth Parliament. The House of Representatives includes seventy-five members, and, like the Senators, they are elected by universal adult suffrage. The members are divided among the states according to population, with a minimum of five members for each state. The distribution is periodically revised and is at present as follows: New South Wales twenty-seven, Victoria twenty-one,

Queensland ten, South Australia seven, Westralia five, Tasmania five. Each Senator and Representative receives an annual allowance of £600, and a seat becomes vacant if the member be absent for two months without leave.

The Senate is probably the most democratic house of Parliament in the world. It consists of six members from each of the six states. Once every three years half the Senators have to seek re-election and each is then elected for six years. The election is by all the residents in a state voting as one constituency. The Senate was thus framed in order to protect the interest of the states against the Federal authority; for each state, no matter what its size or population may be, has equal voting power in the Senate. New South Wales with its population of 1,650,000 has the same representation in the Senate as Tasmania with less than one-eighth the population (191,000). To protect the majority of the people from unfair taxation by a minority which may have secured most of the seats in the Senate, that chamber is not allowed to initiate or amend money bills; but as it is at liberty to suggest amendments to them and can reject a money bill if its suggestions are not accepted, this restriction of its powers appears to be only nominal.

Obstruction by the Senate is restricted by the fact that its power of rejecting bills is limited; if

it twice at an interval of more than three months
reject a bill that has twice passed the House of
Representatives the Governor General may dissolve
both houses of Parliament; and if the new House of
Representatives pass the bill and the Senate again
reject it, the two Houses have to sit together and
the fate of the bill is decided by the majority of the
two Houses. As there are thirty-six Senators and
the Representatives must, according to the Constitution, be twice as many (the number is now
seventy-five), no bill could be permanently rejected
which had the support of a large majority of the
people.

By the irony of circumstance the influence of the
Senate promises to be exactly the opposite of the
intention of its founders; for owing to the method
of election a small majority in each state can elect
all its Senators. There is no representation of
minorities. Thus at the dissolution of 1914 all the
thirty-six Senators were elected and the Labour
party secured thirty-one out of the thirty-six seats.
One of the five Liberal Senators belonging to the
Coalition owed his seat to the death of a Labour
candidate between the nomination and election.
The Labour party generally secures undue representation in the Senate, and as it is anxious to
increase the powers of the Federal Government and
restrict those of the States, the Senate, under present

conditions, is opposed to the very interests it was designed to protect. The upholders of the authority of the States no longer trust the Senate, and occasional conferences of the State Premiers consider the steps necessary to resist projected encroachments of the Federal power.

The authority of an elective Senate has led to great difficulty when there are majorities on opposite sides in the two houses. And the method adopted to avoid political deadlocks has been put to a use which its drafters probably did not contemplate. Thus the Federal Parliament elected in 1900 was divided into three parties—a Protectionist-Liberal party led by Barton and Deakin, a Free Trade party which is generally regarded as also representative of the capitalist and landed interests and was led by Sir George Reid; and the Labour party of which the leader was Mr Watson. The Liberals with the support of the Labour party had a majority and formed the first two administrations. They were succeeded in 1904 by a Labour Government, and in 1904–1905 by a Conservative ministry under Sir George Reid. The Liberals under Deakin, owing to the support of the Labour party, regained office in 1905 and retained it till 1908. The Liberal-Labour Coalition then collapsed as the Labour party insisted on contesting the seats of its Liberal allies. In such three cornered elections the Liberal party had little chance of success, and it would inevitably have lost nearly all its seats. The Liberals under Mr Deakin, therefore, had no option but to form a coalition with the Conservatives, and thus political parties in Australia are now divided into Labour and anti-Labour. The Labour party with Mr Fisher as Prime Minister was in office from 1910 to 1913; but at the general election of 1913 the coalition secured a majority of one in the House of Representatives and took office with Mr Cook as its head. Labour had a strong majority in the Senate. The Senators insist that they, being elected, are as bound in duty to their constituents as the Representatives are to theirs. The Senate accordingly rejected the measures passed by the vote of the odd man in the Lower House. As only half the Senators are elected at each triennial election the Labour majority in the Senate was safe for several years, unless the whole Senate were dissolved under the provision for a double dissolution in the event of a conflict between the two houses.

The Cook ministry therefore twice passed through the House of Representatives a bill for the abolition of preference to trade unionists. The Senate twice rejected it and the Governor General dissolved both Houses. The Labour members complained that this was a breach of the spirit of the Constitution, as they hold that this provision was only intended to apply to serious constitutional questions and not to minor matters of domestic legislation. The Governor General's decision was however clearly in accordance with the letter of the Constitution, and also with commonsense, for it gave the Australian people the chance of ending a complete legislative deadlock by returning to both houses a majority of the same political party. This interesting chapter of Australian political development closed in September 1914 by the return of strong Labour majorities in both houses. In the Senate, the Labour party secured thirty-one out of the thirty-six seats.

Australia is often derided for the retention of the six State Parliaments and it is suggested that it would be wiser to unite into one federal service some of the departments which are still administered independently by the separate States. But considering that Australia is a continent including states in very different geographical conditions, Australia was probably very wise in selecting a Federal Constitution like the United States, instead of a Union Government like South Africa. It is also well advised to maintain separate laws and services for most departments of local administration; for the various parts of the continent are so remote and so dissimilar geographically and politically, that they require very different administrative systems. A Geological Survey of Western Australia for example could not be adequately supervised from Sydney or Melbourne.

Fiscal Policy. The difficulty of framing one policy for the whole of so vast and varied a continent is shown by the growing dissatisfaction in Australia with its fiscal system. This subject illustrates, moreover, how different is the cleavage of political opinion in Australia from that in this country; for the Australian Conservative party is the champion of Free Trade, while the Labour and Radical parties uphold Protection. Before the establishment of the Commonwealth, Victoria was protectionist and the adjacent State of New South Wales adopted Free Trade; and the contrast between the development of the two states was of extreme interest. Victoria had framed a system of scientific protection which was intended to keep the cost of living low by allowing the free import of all necessities; while industries which could be developed in the country were helped by duties, by the advice of official experts or by bounties. Thus cotton goods were imported free to supply cheap clothing; while a high duty was imposed on woollen goods in order to develop the local manufacture of Australian wool. In order to help dairy farmers in the export of butter, experts, at the cost of the State, investigated the bacteriological changes which for a time closed the European markets to butter made on the other side of the tropics. The cause of fishiness in butter having been discovered by the bacteriologists, the export of butter was developed by a bounty. This policy in the special conditions of Victoria was just and judicious. The State stood to gain much by the development of this trade; for its success has caused the subdivision of large sheep runs into dairy farms, and therefore gave more opening for agricultural labour and increased the traffic over the State railways. As the State would receive part of the profit, it was only fair that it should join with the dairy farmers in some share of the risks; and after the butter export had become profitable, the bounty was withdrawn and the trade left to develop without further artificial support.

It has been found impracticable to develop any system of protective duties which is equally helpful to all the Australian states. A duty which helps one State may be useless to another. Accordingly the present fiscal system imposes moderate duties on nearly all articles; it is intended to raise revenue, and it has been vigorously denounced for being inadequately protective. The Commonwealth has given especial protection to certain industries, which, like the northern sugar industry, have been placed under special restrictions, and there appears to be a growing demand in Australia for more effective protection of its young manufactures.

Civil Service. Australia, while following the

example of the United States in the adoption of
a Federal Constitution, has resolutely determined
to prevent any introduction of political interference
with the Civil Service or the administration of the
law. In each of the States the government departments are under a board of Civil Service Commissioners, who are appointed for life and whose
salary cannot be touched by Parliament. They
have the independence and security of High Court
Judges. Moreover, in Victoria at least, the Minister
of a Department has no power of dismissal or even
of giving direct orders to the staff of his Department.
His communications to them must go through the
Secretary of the Department.

The Railways are also under Commissioners, who
are protected as far as possible from political interference. Parliament has of course to decide on the
expenditure of money and the construction of fresh
lines; but to avoid unfair competition between
different localities, proposals for new lines are usually
considered by special expert committees, who may
be trusted to form impartial opinions, and their
recommendations are usually accepted.

There is naturally keen competition between
different localities for State aid in the provision of
roads, railways, schools, irrigation, and mining
prospecting; and each member of Parliament
naturally considers it his duty to lay the needs of

his constituents before the responsible officials. There is no cause for complaint unless the members press local claims unduly. The most serious evil, which affects most elected boards and parliaments that deal only with local administration, is the temptation for the representatives of one district to support demands from another in exchange for support of its own requisitions later on. Such bargaining leads to wasteful and extravagant expenditure, and no doubt Australia could furnish many examples of this procedure. But from direct corruption Australian politics seem exceptionally free.

Labour Party. One remarkable feature in the politics of Australia is the influence of the Labour party, whose power has done much to diminish British confidence in the future of the country. But this distrust is wholly unjust. The Labour party may be mistaken and may be striving after unattainable ideals; but it has a great constructive policy, which is based on present self-sacrifice and is undertaken at the bidding of noble ambitions.

It is difficult to express in a single sentence the aim of any political party, for every party is composed of various groups and is inspired by mixed motives. The moving principle of most large political parties animates probably only a small section of its members, who secure for it the support of a miscellaneous following. Individual observers

usually see or know personally only a small section
of any party, and their impressions vary accordingly.
What to one member of a party may be its essential
creed, may to another be only a secondary item in
its programme, and may appear a canting formula
to its opponents. Thus in Australia while some
observers regard the Labour party as inspired by
generous and far-sighted aims, others regard it as
moved only by the selfishness of men who cannot
see beyond next pay-day.

The principle which underlies the demands of the
Australian Labour party seems to me to be the
conviction that the highest duty of statesmanship is
the development of a high average of national
character. In accordance with that principle the
Labour party insisted on compulsory free education,
the eight hours' day, the provision of good conditions
of work in factories and mines, old age pensions, the
limitation and strict control of the liquor traffic, and
the payment of sufficient wages for the maintenance
of a healthy, comfortable life free from the de-
moralizing influences of abject poverty, insanitary
conditions, and insecurity of work and wage.

All these functions are regarded by most Australians as among the proper duties of the State.
The guardianship of the Government is being continually extended. Thus the public food, which is
very liable to fraudulent adulteration and to injury

by careless preparation, is in Victoria inspected and kept up to standard by an expert committee.

The Australian Labour party striving for these ideals, has recognized the necessity for many measures which the British Labour party regard with horror and dismay. Thus the Labour party recognises that if employers are to pay wages above mere subsistence level, they must be protected from the competition of cheap labour elsewhere; so the Labour party agrees to a protective tariff on imports. It also realizes the need for the defence of the country against direct attack and for security from external enemies without the establishment of a ruling military caste within the state; hence the Labour party has steadily supported universal service for home defence by a citizen army. It has also done more than any other party to establish a powerful Australian navy. It has spent so freely over the army and navy that among all the countries of the world Australia now ranks below only Britain and France in the expenditure per head on national defence (for figures see p. 109).

The Labour party moreover is imperialist. It considers that the British political system offers the best opportunities for the spread of freedom and for peaceful progress; it therefore believes that it is best to remain in the British Empire, and is ready to do its share in the common defence.

The policy of "a White Australia" is also adopted by Labour to avoid the inevitable evils that result from the intermixture of races with altogether different standards of life and morals.

The Labour party, it should be understood, has no monopoly of this programme. Many of the items in it have been passed into law by the Liberals; and men like Deakin, the great Liberal leader and orator, differ from such Labour leaders as Watson and Fisher only over the rate of progress and not over its direction. The Australian Labour movement has however been so widely misunderstood in Britain that its aims need explanation; and, in the interests of Australia as a whole, it is important to make clear that the Labour party, which has so large a share in determining Australian policy, is led by capable statesmen and not by selfish demagogues.

Some advanced Labour members no doubt advocate socialist schemes for the general nationalisation of the means of production; but as all political parties in Australia support the State provision of railways, posts and telegraphs, hospitals, arms-factories and sugar mills, and state contributions to mining development, the nationalisation of special industries involves no new principle. The Labour party shows no intention of adopting any general scheme of industrial nationalisation. Its proposals have been directed against special trusts and corporations which have been suspected of striving to establish tyrannous or dangerous monopolies. The nationalisation of any such monopoly would be consistent with the policy supported at one time or another by all Australian parties.

The Coalition Party. To summarize the policy of the other political party is difficult, as it is a coalition of two groups which have very different ideas. Its central section is the Free Trade party, which held that, under existing conditions, the best policy for Australia is the production of raw materials; it approved of free trade so as to reduce the cost of living and of production. Any attempt to carry out this policy has apparently been abandoned as hopeless; and the Free Traders have combined with a section of Protectionists, with whom the chief point in common is opposition to the Labour party.

The Coalitionists regard the Labour party as naturally careless in expenditure since the taxation is mostly paid by the wealthier classes; they think that it is drifting towards an extreme socialism which will impoverish Australia by sapping industrial effort, that it is prepared to sacrifice the industrial progress of Australia to the ease and comfort of the workers, and that it is ready to maintain Australia as a paradise of the artisan by artificial maintenance of high wages and a small labour supply. Nevertheless there appear to be no big direct issues between the two parties. The bitter conflict between the Federal elections of 1913 and 1914 was over details; the longest dispute was over the respective merits of the postal vote and the absentee vote, which is a small question of electoral machinery. This issue was dropped at the last moment, and the question on which both houses of parliament were dissolved was over preference to trades-unionists; but the preference involved was so restricted as to be only of secondary importance. As the two opposing parties are not divided by any clear fundamental principle, Australian political differences are becoming more and more a matter of class distinctions.

The division between Liberal and Conservative in British politics is based on impersonal general principles, the adoption of which is determined by temperament and intellectual sympathies. This division cuts across all social and class distinctions. The issue of Labour against Capital on the other hand divides a country into groups, which are separated by class interests; and this division is apt to lead to more selfish views. For the unfortunate political subdivision of Australia on these narrow class lines, the Labour party is chiefly responsible, owing to its refusal to cooperate with the Liberals at the Federal elections.

Future of Australian Parliamentary Government. Australia has so often been the pioneer in political experiments that it is of interest to consider what light the recent developments in Australia throw on the future of parliamentary government.

The old British system has been greatly modified in Australian practice, owing to the increase in the power of the Caucus or party machine. The Labour party elects its leader, and when he is called on to form a Ministry, his colleagues are elected by the party and not selected by the Prime Minister. The party as a whole decides in secret conclave what bills shall be passed and determines their scope. The Labour members discuss the measures in private, and may in Parliament leave the explanation and defence of the bill entirely to the minister in charge, and they may attend only to record silent votes in its favour. Under such a system Parliament is not a deliberative assembly, but a voting place. Machinery is made in it for carrying out the policy that has been discussed elsewhere and has been informally approved by the country. The change is deplored by many as inconsistent with true parliamentary government. The tendency is however also noticeable in the British House of Commons where the Cabinet tends to become an omnipotent caucus; and Parliament has been equally ignored in debate, as when the advocates of the Scottish Temperance Act of 1913 passed it in silence since, owing to shortness of time, discussion would have been fatal to the measure.

The self-management of a party in full though secret conference appears more in harmony with the principles of representative government than the supremacy of a group of autocrats.

CHAPTER VIII

THE AUSTRALIAN BUDGET

The revenues of Australia include the income of the Commonwealth and of the States.   The Commonwealth collects all the Customs and Excise, but returns part of it to each state in proportion to its contributions.

The Commonwealth revenue for 1911–12 was £20,548,520 or £4. 9s. 11d. per head of the population. Customs contributed £12,071,434, the post-office £3,916,254 and the land tax on unimproved land £1,366,457.   The Commonwealth expenditure for the same year was £14,724,097 or £3. 4s. 6d. per head. The most expensive Federal service is the post-office which cost £4,330,896 so that it was conducted at a loss of £414,642; but considering the conditions in the back country, the only wonder is that so cheap and excellent a service can be given at so slight an expense.   Defence cost £2,128,649, more than double the amount of the previous year.

The balance of £5,824,423 of the Federal Revenue over Expenditure was returned to the six States.

The Commonwealth Government has a small debt. In June 1912 it was £6,371,847; of this £5,671,000 was due to liabilities on the Northern Territory and on the South Australian railway from Port Augusta to Oodnadatta, which were assumed by the Commonwealth from South Australia on the cession of the Northern Territory.

The States revenues for 1911–12 are as follows:

	£	Per head of population £ s. d.
New South Wales	15,776,816	9 8 5
Victoria	10,009,796	7 6 11
Queensland ...	5,989,347	9 12 6
South Australia ...	4,450,739	10 12 10
Westralia... ...	3,966,673	13 9 8
Tasmania ...	1,084,663	5 12 1
Total for Commonwealth ...	£41,278,034	£9 0 8

Of the State revenues 13·13 per cent. are derived from taxation, including a moderate income tax, probate and succession duties and stamp duties; 57·39 per cent. comes from public works, of which by far the most important are the railway receipts, though water supply is also important; 9·58 per cent. is paid in land taxes; 14·19 per cent. from the Federal subsidy and 5·71 per cent. is miscellaneous.

The expenditure of the six States in 1911–12 was

£40,858,581 or £8. 18s. 10d. per head.   The expenditure is subdivided as follows:

	£	
Charges on the State debts ...	10,879,267	= 60 per cent.
Working of railways and trains	13,665,906	
Education	3,593,620	= 8·79 per cent.
Police and justice	2,203,979	
Medical and charitable ...	1,821,298	
Miscellaneous	8,704,511	

The public debts of the States were in 1912:

	£	Per head of population £ s. d.
New South Wales	100,052,635	57 11 9
Victoria	60,737,216	44 16 11
Queensland ...	47,068,186	74 5 0
South Australia ...	31,680,124	75 5 8
Westralia ...	26,283,523	86 18 8
Tasmania ...	11,302,411	59 9 7
	£277,124,095	

The State and Federal debts together amount to over £60 per head, and it appears at first sight a very heavy burden, especially as only Westralia has a full sinking fund by which loans are automatically repaid. The charge on the credit of Australia is the less serious as by far the largest proportion of the debt has been spent on railways, harbour works and water supply, all of which are directly remunerative and mostly yield a profit on their full cost; much of the remainder of the debt has been spent on schools and public buildings which are indirectly remunerative.

CHAPTER IX

THE DEFENCE OF AUSTRALIA

Australia until 1870 was garrisoned by British troops. After their withdrawal the different colonies organized bodies of volunteers and subsequently of militia. The harbours were defended by small forces of permanent artillery, by flotillas of torpedo boats and some gun boats. The efficiency of the Australian troops was shown by the contingents sent to the Sudan in 1885, and to South Africa in 1899 to 1902[1]. In 1900 the defence of Australia became one of the main duties of the young Commonwealth; and it has organized a national army in which universal service is compulsory, supplemented by a small permanent force managed by a permanent staff. The citizen army is to include every able-bodied man belonging to the European races, with

[1] The supreme courage and efficiency of the Australian troops has been shown still more strikingly by their magnificent conduct at Gallipoli, and *Punch's* poem "The bravest thing God ever made" is a well merited tribute to the heroism of the Australian troops in that glorious but ill-fated campaign. The value of the Australian fleet was also shown by the destruction of the *Emden* by the *Sydney*, and the important part played by the battle cruiser *Australia* in the pursuit of the German cruiser squadron which was finally destroyed off the Falklands.

the exception of residents in remote districts and men engaged in a few special employments, such as doctors and lighthouse-keepers. Those who could satisfy the authorities that they had genuine conscientious objections to bearing arms were at first excused from serving in the fighting line, but were required to give an equivalent amount of service in the non-combatant branches of the army.

Citizen Army. Preparations for a citizen army had been initiated in Victoria by the educational authorities. Sir Frederick Sargood, when Minister for Education, established school cadet corps, and military drill has long been compulsory in the Victorian State schools. This system has been extended by the Act of 1909. All boys are drilled as cadets at the expense of the Defence Department by school teachers who have been trained by the military staff. The junior cadets are from 12 to 14 years of age and they have ninety hours drill a year. Senior cadets are from 14 to 18 years old, and they have to attend annually twenty-four night classes, twelve half days and four full days. Rifle Clubs supported by the Government afford opportunities for practice in shooting. From the age of 18 to 36 men are enrolled in the citizen army, and have to give sixteen days training in camp; they are paid for this time at rates varying from 4*s*. a day for a private to £2. 5*s*. a day for a colonel;

so that a colonel during peace receives £36 a year. The members of the force engaged for full time include the general staff, regiments of engineers, field and garrison artillery, medical and army service corps. As the army scheme is young the forces are still incomplete. In 1913 the permanent soldiers numbered 2774, the reserve of officers 914, the senior cadets 88,708, the members of official rifle clubs 50,000 and the citizen forces, 31,000, a total of 174,000 men; but under this system in a few years' time the whole manhood of Australia will have been trained to the use of arms and form an army of 700,000 men.

Naval Service. The naval defence of the six colonies was begun by arrangements for coast and harbour defence by gun boats, torpedo boats, mine fields, and corps of naval volunteers. With the growing strength of Russia as an eastern power and the rise of the Pacific problems, these local independent services were regarded as inadequate. The Imperial Government therefore undertook in 1890 to provide a cruiser squadron and some torpedo-boats, for which Australia paid an annual contribution of £12,600. In 1903 the squadron was strengthened and included a first class cruiser, and the Australian subsidy was raised to half the cost, or £200,000. The Australian proposal that it should organize an independent service was declined, as in

deference to a formula that the sea is one and
indivisible, a small naval squadron absolutely under
the British Admiralty was preferred to a stronger
force under Australian management. This decision
delayed the growth of Australian interest in naval
affairs.

In 1909 this policy was reversed and Australia
undertook to provide a naval force adequate for the
protection of its own coasts and coastal trade. Its
navy now consists of a powerful battleship—the
Australia—, three cruisers, various torpedo destroyers,
torpedo boats and submarines; according to the
scheme adopted the fleet will consist by 1918 of
twenty-three vessels and its total is to be over fifty.

Expenditure on Defence. The total expenditure
for defence in 1913–14 is estimated at £5,750,000.
The cost of naval and military services per head of
the population in various countries is as follows:

		£	s.	d.
Great Britain	...	1	12	3
France ...	...	1	8	7
Australia ...	...	1	3	7
Germany ...	...	1	1	5
Italy ...	...		12	9
United States	...		12	0
Austro-Hungary	...		7	6
Canada ...	...		4	5

Hence Australia ranks third in its military and
naval expenditure per head of the population and

considering its remote and inaccessible position, the
difficulty of attacking it, the necessity for spending
great sums on development, and the fact that the
opening of its empty northern spaces by railways and
immigration would be its surest protection, Australia
cannot be fairly charged with being niggardly in its
expenditure on defence.   It seems clear that Australia has adopted the policy which will enable her
to make best use of her military resources and give
the most effective support to the Empire by maintaining British influence in the Pacific and south-
eastern Asia.

The Australian citizen army includes many novel
features, varying from details such as the prohibition
of the sale of intoxicating liquors at the military
camps, to the fundamental principle of saving the
time of the adults by training them as cadets, when
their time is far less valuable.   According to General
Sir Ian Hamilton, this feature in the Australian
plan promises success.   "Strange indeed will it be,"
he remarks in his report on his Inspection of the
Australian army, "if a country in which no wars
have yet been waged, should at its first serious
attempt hit the nail on the head ! "..."Australia may
yet...boast that she has shown the way...of raising
powerful armies for home defence with a minimum
tax on the priceless time of the adult male worker."...
"The striking success achieved wherever environment

has happened to be favourable is evidence that Australia is really in the right track, and that the difficulties she is experiencing are only the small but distressing hitches which have taken place in the earlier stages of every and any great invention. If the Empire understood the full significance of this Australian experiment, prayers would continually be in process of being offered up in the churches for its success."

CHAPTER X

LAND TENURE

Batman the founder of Melbourne and one of the earliest settlers in Victoria made a treaty with the aborigines which assigned to himself and his associates the ownership of a large tract of land around Melbourne in exchange for an annual payment of commodities. To his disappointment this treaty was disallowed on the ground that all Australia is crown land, and the only valid title is a grant by the British Government. Free grants were nominally abolished in 1831, except for educational purposes, parks, recreation reserves and water supply; but land has steadily passed into the possession of

private owners, by various methods of lease and
purchase.

Australia had the opportunity of retaining the
national proprietorship of all its land; and as less
than eight per cent. is private property, this policy
could still be adopted for nine-tenths of the continent.

The State has parted with land permanently by
various methods of purchase and temporarily by
various forms of lease. Land is sold outright for
farms and homesteads; and on "conditional purchase," which is only completed on the fulfilment of
various stipulations such as clearing for settlement,
drainage, irrigation, or the eradication of various
imported pests such as prickly pear. The rate at
which land is now passing into private ownership
may be illustrated by the following list for 1911.
New South Wales, 8127 acres; Victoria, 4068 acres;
Queensland, 10,123 acres; South Australia, 470,000
acres; Tasmania, 190 acres; while in the same year
by conditional purchase, New South Wales disposed
of 671,000 acres, Queensland of 1,741,000 (of which
over one million was land infected by prickly pear and
was sold at 5s. 2½d. an acre conditionally on clearance
of this scourge), and Westralia 1,923,000 acres.
Hence the total land sold outright or conditionally
in 1911 was 4,828,400 acres. The purchase price of
such land is usually paid in annual instalments which
may be spread over many years.

Most of the Australian land occupied is held on various forms of lease or license; the lessees often have the right of conditional purchase, and land on these terms is usually held on a forty years lease. In New South Wales, over 15,500,000 acres are thus let at an average rent of 3*d*. per acre; in Westralia the land leased amounts to 74,750,000 acres, at an average annual rent of three acres for 1*d*. The total for Australia is nearly 126,000,000 acres which brings in a total annual rent of £568,000. Although such large areas are let on lease or are still unoccupied, there is more difficulty than would be at first expected, at any rate in Victoria and New South Wales, in providing fresh settlers with cheap suitable land; for newcomers and men with small capital require land of good quality and accessible to a market. Much of the best land passed early into private hands and was used for great sheep stations; and in suitable districts as on the western plains of Victoria some of the sheep runs have been converted by the proprietors into dairy farms on a partnership system. The owner provides the land, builds a butter factory, and may supply the cattle; the tenant furnishes the labour and pays his rent in a percentage of cream which he sends to the factory. In other cases the State has repurchased estates, and subdivided them into farms. The areas thus acquired by the States for closer settlement up to June 1912 are as follows:

	acres	
New South Wales	676,438	
Victoria	515,604	
Queensland ...	664,363	(to end of 1911)
South Australia ...	619,469	
Westralia ...	303,469	
Tasmania ...	41,150	

The proportions of land alienated by the States, of that under lease and of that still unoccupied are stated in the following table, which shows that in 1911 ninety-two per cent. of Australia was still national property:

	Land alienated or in process of alienation %	Land under license and lease %	Unoccupied or occupied by crown %	Total area of State in mill. of acres
New South Wales ...	27·66	62·04	10·30	198
Victoria	53·49	26·34	20·17	56¼
Queensland ...	5·76	71·82	22·42	429
South Australia ...	4·79	45·67	49·54	243¼
Westralia	3·34	28·13	68·53	624½
Tasmania	37·20	9·05	53·75	16¾
Northern Territory	·14	27·97	71·89	335
Whole Commonwealth	7·74	43·20	49·06	1902¾

Whether land should be sold outright or the ownership kept by the state has been the subject of prolonged discussion, especially in recent years with reference to the Northern Territory. Owing to the influence of the Labour party, it has been decided to let the land there on lease only. The view is often expressed that this decision will greatly delay the development of that territory. This result does not however seem inevitable. Until 1912 land could be purchased in the Northern Territory; so the leasehold policy is not responsible for the slow progress in the past. As the Australian pastoral industry has been mainly and the mining industry almost entirely developed on leasehold property, past experience in Australia does not support the view that people would decline to accept land on lease if a profit could be made out of it.

CHAPTER XI

INDUSTRIAL AND SOCIAL LEGISLATION

Owing to the special geographical conditions of Australia its governments were forced from the beginning to adopt a somewhat socialistic policy. Of the six States three were founded as penal settlements; another—South Australia—was begun as an experiment in colonisation, under a management, which, though philanthropic, was as arbitrary and absolute as that over the convicts. Accordingly various enterprises which in this country have been left to private companies were necessarily undertaken by the State Governments. The early tendency to patriarchal and socialistic government

8—2

was strengthened by various geographical influences when, after the discovery of the gold mines in 1851, Australia first began to increase rapidly in population and prosperity.

State Railways. The gold-fields are in the interior and were discovered at a time when, owing to the scantiness of the population, all the energies of the people were occupied in developing the mines and supplying the miners with their various necessities. There was no private capital available for railway development, and it is doubtful whether private investors would then have risked money on railway construction in Australia except at exorbitant interest.

The first important Australian railway was from Melbourne to the mining field of Bendigo. It cost the appalling sum of £48,000 a mile. Wages were high and the bricklayers in Melbourne are said to have then driven to their work every morning in cabs. The mining fields were widely scattered and as they were mainly in mountainous districts the cost of railways leading to them was necessarily high. Railway communication was however a national necessity and the nation accepted the duty of supplying it. Similar conditions held with the agricultural development. Vast areas in the interior would still be unoccupied, if they had had to wait for railways until their construction was commercially profitable. Railways are being built in Australia which, according to an oft used phrase, will not pay for their axle grease for a couple of generations. Some Australian railways have no immediate chance of paying interest on their cost, unless the kangaroos take season tickets.

The railways of the Commonwealth in 1912 amounted to a total length of 18,653 miles including 1755 miles of private lines; nearly half the latter are timber and mining lines not open for public traffic. In reference to population there is one mile of railway to 457 people in New South Wales; to 372 in Victoria; to 287 in Tasmania; to 216 in South Australia; to 105 in Westralia; and to 23 in the Northern Territory. The gauges used vary from 5 ft 3 in., which was originally selected as the standard gauge, to 1 ft. 8 in., which is used for some special lines. There are 4222 miles of the 5 ft 3 in. gauge in Victoria and South Australia; 4013 miles of the 4 ft 8½ in. gauge, all in New South Wales; and 10,099 miles of the 3 ft 6 in. gauge nearly all in Queensland, South Australia and Westralia; and 343 miles of smaller gauges.

The construction of the early Australian railways was very costly. The Bendigo Railway, 100 miles long, cost £4,800,000; but in recent years railways have been built at very moderate cost; 5 ft 3 in. railways have been made in the Mallee country of north-west Victoria at the cost of only £1500 per mile. The railways are now worked at a profit; the gross revenue of the whole of the railways in 1911–12 was £19,101,000; the total working expenses for the same year was £12,471,000; the interest on loan expenditure was £5,650,000 leaving a balance of £980,000 as profit after paying all expenses and interest. The profit is only ·61 per cent. on the capital, which as a commercial return would be too low; the railways, however, are not run to make dividends, but to develop the country.

The railways might no doubt have been built by private enterprise with a government guarantee. But the Australian governments however thought that if they had to incur the financial risks, they might as well secure for the country the ultimate profits; and in spite of the extent to which non-paying railway lines have been built to develop remote districts, the railway system as a whole has justified the foresight of its founders by more than paying its expenses. The profit would be greater were it not for the policy that, as soon as the railways yield a considerable surplus, new lines are built for development purposes. The financial success of the railways is all the more remarkable because they have to bear the burden of all the unprofitable lines and of the occasional mistakes which are inevitable in so great an undertaking. America left the building

of her back country lines to private companies,
and when one of them had spent its capital it made
a fresh start by mortgaging the line. The working
of some American railways has been maintained by
second, third and fourth mortgages; so that such
railways now only pay interest on a small fraction
of their cost. The Australian railways have to pay
for all time the full interest upon every pound spent
on them, and they will always be burdened by the
high cost of construction in the early days. Australia
has however the consolation of knowing that it has
adopted the most honest way of providing itself with
railways.

Australian experience throws little light on the
problems whether it would have been better in other
countries for the government to have supplied the
railways, and whether their nationalisation now
would be a wise step. Australian opinion is still
divided as to whether its railway system would be
better under private control. The most frequent
complaint against the railway administration is that
the management shows lack of elasticity in dealing
with the public and in refusal to concede specially
low rates in such cases as the carriage of fertilizers,
where any concessions would be well repaid by the
increased transport receipts from the larger harvests.
The most serious charge against the railway administration is that, owing to the lack of competition

between rival companies, the railway system has helped to concentrate the trade of each State in its capital, and to block the development of local centres and independent ports. But after having travelled extensively over the Australian railways and also over those of Canada and the United States my own feeling is that Australia has done well to keep the railways in the hands of the Governments.

Mining Laws. Respecting the mining laws of Australia we hear two sharply opposed views. According to some investors, the mining law developed by the old Boer Government in the Transvaal was the best in the world and the Australian is the worst. Recent American opinion on Australian mining laws adopts what seems to me a much juster view, and regards the Australian mining legislation, as on the whole the best that has yet been developed. The recent report by Veitch of the United States Geological Survey gives warm testimony to the wisdom of the Australian mining policy. The two fundamental principles of Australian mining legislation are that the minerals belong to the State and that instead of parting with the freehold of the minerals the State will only grant leases, so as to ensure that the mines are worked properly and in accordance with certain "labour covenants." Foreign investors especially object to the refusal of freeholds and the insistence on these labour covenants.

The principle of Australian mining policy is that
though the State owns the minerals, it does not tax
the output and is content with indirect returns.
The lessee has to pay small fees for survey and
registration and sometimes a nominal rent.   As the
State leases public property to a private company
it fairly insists that that company must work the
lease, and must employ a specified amount of labour.
The State obtains its return by the settlement of a
larger population in the mining district, by the gain
to the national wealth, and by increased railway
receipts.

The labour covenants have not been unjustly or
unduly pressed. If for any good reason a mine has
temporarily to cease work, exemption from the
labour clauses of its lease are given by the Minister
of Mines.   But if a company is compelled to stop
work through incompetence, or tries to postpone
working the property until its neighbours have
developed the district, then anyone can apply for
the forfeiture of the lease, which may be granted to
some one who will promise to fulfil its conditions.

Labour Legislation. The section of Australian
politics of probably the widest general interest is
that dealing with the care of labour.   It was early
recognized by Australian statesmen that the labourers
must be helped and carefully guarded from oppres-
sion.   Artisans in Australia were at first in many

respects more defenceless than they were in the British Isles. Each of the States began with a settlement, which is now its chief town and from which the whole State has been developed and administered. The relations of the capital to the provinces are quite different from those in Europe. All England for example was occupied before it had a capital. London was a fishing village much smaller than many contemporary British towns, until under the Romans it became a chief administrative and commercial centre. In Australia on the other hand the capitals were founded first and the country was occupied and administered from off-shoots of the capitals. Hence they have always held a share of the population and a commercial administrative influence which, judged by European standards, appear excessive. Thus thirty-eight per cent. of the population of New South Wales live in and around Sydney and forty-five per cent. of the Victorians live in Melbourne and its suburbs. Accordingly the capitalists of each State are collected in one centre, while the labourers are dispersed through the country and are in a less favourable position for organization. In consequence of the special geographical conditions of Australia there is unusually little competition among the employers, while the workmen are handicapped by their inability, if discharged in one city to remove to another and obtain employment there,

The Government early recognized the need for
helping the labourers, who themselves saw the need
for developing their own unions. It was early
admitted in Australia by members of all political
parties and all classes that it is the first duty of
Government to prevent the degeneration of character
by blighting poverty and overwork. There is nothing
revolutionary in this doctrine for one of its most
influential advocates in England was Disraeli.
According to William Morris "the chief duty of the
civilized world to-day is to set about making labour
happy for all, to do its utmost to minimize the
amount of unhappy labour." The adoption of the
"three eights" as the first item on the programme of
the Australian Labour party was an important step
towards fulfilling this duty. The "three eights"
means division of the day into eight hours for work,
eight hours for rest, and eight hours for recreation.
The eight hours' day has been adopted in Australia
for most of the large, well organized industries.
Eight hours having been allotted for recreation it
was necessary that opportunities should be provided
for their profitable use. Hence provision was made
for reading rooms, museums, and picture galleries;
and the growth of well-informed and cheap news-
papers was encouraged by giving them cheap
distribution by post and railway. To prevent the
liquor trade profiting too greatly by the eight hours

for recreation, Australia has adopted, with the
support of the Labour party, a very advanced
policy for the control and limitation of the trade
in drink. Thus Sunday closing is rigidly enforced;
the number of licences is restricted; and the State
has thus aided the reduction in the consumption of
alcohol and the adoption of tea as the national
beverage of Australia[1].

Education. An advanced educational policy was
also recognized as indispensable for the success of
the democratic programme. Education throughout
Australia is compulsory, free, and non-sectarian.
Compulsory education amongst the sparsely scattered
population of the back blocks of Australia must be
difficult and costly. I remember my surprise shortly
after I went to Australia, at finding a State school
in a locality where there were only two settlers.
I roughly calculated the cost of that school and the
rate per child seemed extravagant. After returning
to Melbourne, I remarked to the Director of Education that it would be much cheaper for the State to
pay for a private tutor to the two families. He
replied that the provision of such schools was
essential to the land settlement policy of the State

---

[1] The consumption of beer per head in Australia is less than half
that of the British Isles, and the quantity of spirits used is slightly
less; the rate of wine consumption is nearly twice as great, but its
amount in proportion to the beer is insignificant.

and their cost should be charged against land settlement and not against the ordinary education rate. The pioneers on the outskirts of settlement, must, to be successful, have foresight and imagination. Inadaptive, unintelligent workers would fail and discourage the advance of settlement; and good settlers are the very people who will not handicap their children by placing them where they cannot obtain a sound education. Hence the high cost per head of the back country schools is fully justified.

The policy of Australia in dealing with its Universities has also been remarkably generous and far seeing and has been maintained by all the political parties. One of the main acts of the recent Labour Government in New South Wales was the great extension of Sydney University. The government arranged for the University to control through its examinations the whole secondary education of the State; and a greatly increased grant has been given to the University on condition that it is open freely to any individual in the State who wishes to attend. Provision has been made for free exhibitions at the University to the number of one for every 500 of the people of New South Wales between 17 and 20 years of age; and the subsidy to the University is to be increased if a larger proportion take advantage of this privilege.

This policy has been adversely criticized on the

ground that it will tend to increase unduly the
technical and professional sides of the University
at the expense of its purely academic branches of
work.   This development is probably inevitable in
Australia, where the number of those who can afford
to devote several years to education solely for
culture is very limited.   Only the wealthy can
afford this luxury and they usually send their sons
to British Universities, as a suitable opportunity for
a visit to Europe.   Australian Universities tend
naturally to grow into great professional schools.
This is however no educational disadvantage, provided the work be maintained at a high standard;
for culture and the principles of science can be taught
at least as well by the study of those subjects which
are of practical value, as of those in which the
interest is purely theoretical.

   Industrial Peace and Minimum Wage.   The
Australian political experiments which are probably
of most general interest are those for securing industrial peace and fixing a living wage by law.
When the evils of sweating began to appear in
Australia, special legislation was suggested to prevent the establishment there of the demoralising
poverty of the great cities of Europe and America.
It was felt that it ought to be possible to govern a
land with such immense natural resources as Australia, so that any man who would do a good day's

work should receive sufficient wages to enjoy a
healthy and comfortable life. The difficulties in
enforcing such a policy are with industries which
cannot pay a living wage and with selfish employers
who will not. Victoria took the lead boldly and
accepted the doctrine that it is as much the duty
of the state to ensure that its artisans enjoy a living
wage, as it is to secure them good air in mine and
factory, and that the state is as much bound to
protect the working classes from fraud in food and
wages as from ordinary burglary. Fixing wages by
act of Parliament is however a step that leads to so
many others, such as the prohibition of industrial
war, that some critics of this policy declare it must
lead to industrial destruction.

A fixed minimum wage will inflict some hardship
on the inefficient. An employer cannot be expected
to pay the full wage of a competent worker to one
who through physical or mental infirmity is not
worth it. Accordingly, that the less fit may not be
thrust out of employment, the Victorian regulations
allow an exemption to be given by the Minister to
any workman certified as inefficient. These certificates have been freely given, but they do not prevent
some cases of suffering to the infirm. Some employers who would not discharge an old workman
will not make the necessary effort to retain him,
because he makes less profitable use of their space

and capital.   Employers also object to the increased
supervision which follows the employment of men
under these certificates of incompetency; and they
run the risk of fine for infringement of the law if
the workman forgets to renew his certificate.   Other
employers object to engaging men with exemption
certificates for fear of popular misrepresentation,
for they may be accused of paying less than the
legal minimum wage by those, who are ignorant of
the fact that these special rates have been officially
sanctioned.

It appears therefore that the minimum wage on
the whole tends to injure the less competent work
people, though it seems impossible to devise any
system by which the inefficient can be more fairly
treated than by the exemption certificate.

The establishment of a minimum wage and the
prohibition of strikes and lock-outs have been
attempted in Australia by two different methods—
Wages Boards, which were founded by Victoria in
1896 in order to stop sweating, and Compulsory
Arbitration.   The essential difference between these
methods is that arbitration refers a trade dispute to
a neutral party, who generally has no special knowledge of the trade and may not understand the
technical difficulties in the dispute he is asked to
settle.   The Wages Board, or other form of Conciliation Board, is on the other hand composed

of the actual disputants. All of them are experts in the trade and they argue the question out amongst themselves. The board consists of equal numbers of employers and employed. There is generally a neutral chairman; and if he has a vote he is practically an arbitrator. For one period during the operation of the Victorian Wages Board, namely in 1902 and 1903, the vote of the chairman was abolished, so that no agreement could be arrived at, if employers and employed voted solidly for their respective sides. The modification was apparently not a success, and the vote of the chairman was restored in 1903.

The advantages claimed for the Wages Board System are that it secures for the labourer a fair wage; it protects the honest employer from selfish competitors, and helps him by lessening the danger of strikes and by determining for some time ahead the exact cost for labour. Further, as in the Conferences employers and employed sit together, they both learn the other side's point of view and realize its difficulties. These meetings should therefore engender mutual respect and confidence. Counsel are not allowed to plead for either side, so progress is not delayed by long explanatory speeches. The Boards are elastic and informal in their procedure, which is inexpensive.

Much no doubt depends on the chairman, who

has the odd vote.   He is appointed by the Governor
from some independent class.   I was, for example,
once appointed chairman of the Wages Board in the
wood-working trade; but I did not serve, as at that
time the position of these boards was giving rise to
some political controversy, and it was thought
inexpedient for a member of the University staff
to take part in their administration.

In Victoria fifty-two boards had been appointed
by 1908 and they covered two-thirds of the industries
of the State.   The largest boards were those dealing
with clothing, baking, furniture manufacture, and
printing.

The Wages Boards can settle disputes as to
industrial regulations, but their main function has
been to fix a minimum wage.   In most cases in
which the boards have had to decide wages, the rate
has been increased, because it was mainly in the
underpaid trades in which appeals were made to the
boards.

There has been prolonged discussion as to the
effect of the Wages Boards.   The employees have
been disappointed at the comparatively small increase in wages, while a few of the employers have
declared that the wages have been unduly raised.
The reports of the general body of employers, however, show that there has been no great increase
of wages as a result of the decisions of the boards.

The opinion of most impartial observers is that
their influence has been to check undue competition,
to prevent sweating, and to raise wages that were
far below the average, but not to affect appreciably
the wages of the better paid and skilled artisans.
They have increased the use of machinery in some
trades. According to the interesting report by
Mr Aves, who visited Australia on behalf of the
British Board of Trade to report upon the working
of Wages Boards, they have not materially raised
the cost of production. They have unquestionably
not prevented the industrial development of Victoria.
It appears clear, moreover, that they have lessened
trade disputes, and local opinion both among
employers and employed is that the Wages Board
system has been much more successful in securing
industrial peace than has the system of compulsory
arbitration.

Compulsory Arbitration has been tried in New
South Wales and by the Commonwealth. New South
Wales has had most experience of this system, which
was established there in 1901. Up till 1904 most
of my mining friends in New South Wales thought
the Act had been upon the whole a success; for
though they recognized that it would not compel
people to work for a lower wage than they could
gain in other industries and could not force an employer to work a mine which had ceased to pay, the

Act had stopped a number of those small disputes which irritate both sides and sometimes lead to disastrous strikes or lock-outs. In recent years, in spite of the Act, there have been several serious strikes, and most of the employers apparently regard compulsory arbitration as a failure. They say that though the award can be enforced against them, there is no practical method of enforcing it against the employees.

The New South Wales Government has certainly done its best to enforce the laws impartially against both sides. When the coal miners struck in 1909 the police broke up the strike meetings and imprisoned the unionist leaders; one of them was sentenced to twelve months imprisonment. The Government intervention stopped the strike and thus showed that the law could be enforced against labour as well as against capital.

A census of local opinion as held by both employers and employed regarding the working of the two systems was taken by Mr Aves. He found that in Victoria of the employees six thought the Wages Board system had improved the relations of employers and employed, two that it had impaired them, and four that it had left them unaffected. Of the employers, however, nine thought that it had improved conditions, nineteen that it had impaired them, and thirteen that it had left them unaffected.

Of independent observers in Victoria, six thought industrial relations had been improved by the Wages Boards and only one that relations had been impaired.

In answer to his question whether the Wages Board system was superior or inferior to Compulsory Arbitration, none of the New South Wales employers regarded Compulsory Arbitration as the better, but the employees were unanimous in preferring Compulsory Arbitration. In Victoria, however, where the Wages Boards were in operation, eighteen of the employees thought them better than Compulsory Arbitration, three thought them inferior, and two were doubtful. Of the independent observers in Victoria the whole thirteen thought the Wages Board the better system.

Mr Aves' report further shows that the employers by nearly two to one regarded the system of allowing inefficient workmen to work below the minimum wage under certificate, as unsatisfactory; the employees were almost equally divided in their opinion for and against it.

New Zealand tried to combine both the conciliation and arbitration systems in one act, which was drafted in 1891 by Sir Pember Reeves, and was carried in 1894. By this Act an industrial dispute is first referred to a Conciliation Board, and if that cannot agree it passes the case on to the Arbitration

Court. It was expected that nearly every dispute
would be settled by the Conciliation Boards; but
they practically failed. It was found that neither
side would state the whole of its case to the conciliation board; for if no agreement were reached
there, the side which had announced all its evidence
would be at a disadvantage during the subsequent
fight in the law courts. Hence an amending Act in
1900 enabled the dispute to be referred at once to
an Arbitration Court.

Westralia, in 1911, in the last of the leading
Australian Arbitration acts, has however, followed
to some extent the New Zealand principle of com-
bining both systems. This Act shows that Australians are still confident that compulsory arbitration may be successful. The Act controls wages,
hours of work, conditions of employment of children
and young persons, regulations for apprenticeship,
etc. It arranges for the establishment of associations
of both employers and employed; and it can refuse
registration and the privileges of the Act amongst
other grounds, to any association which does not
provide reasonable facilities for the admission of
new members, or which imposes unreasonable or
oppressive conditions upon any members of the
association. The Act allows associations of employers
and workers to decide any industrial dispute or
industrial matter; but if the associations of employer

and employed cannot come to a decision, then the
question is referred to the Court of Arbitration,
which is composed of three members, one representative of each side and a Supreme Court Judge who
is nominated by the Governor and is President of
the Court.   This Court may determine any industrial
dispute which is referred to it by any party under
the act, or by the President of the Court, if no agreement can be reached by a conference between the
two parties.

There have been some difficulties as for instance
over the bakers' strike in Melbourne, owing to a Court
giving a decision on technical legal grounds, which
were generally felt to be inequitable.   The judge in
that case said he could only decide on the evidence
before him, and the employees refused to give evidence because, they declared, any witnesses on their
side would be marked men.   The workmen said that
the judge should obtain independent evidence and
use his common sense.   The judge however decided
the case on the evidence legally before him.   But
his verdict proved futile, for the men struck, and
as the public supported the men, the masters, in
spite of their legal victory, had to give way.   To
avoid this difficulty section 54 of the Western
Australia Act decrees that:

"In the hearing and determination of every
industrial dispute the Court or President shall act

according to equity, good conscience, and the substantial merits of the case without regard to technicalities or legal forms, and shall not be bound by any rules of evidence, but may inform its or his mind on the matter in such a way as it or he thinks just."

The Court may award a minimum wage, prescribe rules for the regulation of any industry, and limit the hours of piece workers in any industry except the agricultural and pastoral industries. The Act defines a minimum wage as follows:

"No minimum rate of wages or other remuneration shall be prescribed which is not sufficient to enable the average worker to whom it applies to live in reasonable comfort, having regard to any domestic obligations to which such average worker would be ordinarily subject."

The Court has power to enforce its awards by fine and to secure the fines may seize the property of any industrial union or association. The Act prohibits strikes or lock-outs, and imposes a fine of £100 for breach of this regulation by any employer, union or association, or of £10 in other cases. The Act allows the suspension or discontinuance of work or employment on either side for any good cause independent of any industrial dispute; but it prohibits the suspension of either work or employment in consequence of a dispute, until a reasonable time has elapsed for reference of the matter to the Court.

This Westralian act strives therefore to combine conciliation and arbitration; but it does not appear to overcome the difficulty that has been hitherto found in all compulsory arbitration, of enforcing its award on the employees.

Although compulsory arbitration does not stop all strikes, it may be of value; and in spite of many disappointments Australia seems no more prepared to abandon legislation against strikes because it does not always prevent them, than it is prepared to rescind the statutes against theft because some men still thieve. The greatest difficulty which confronts all such legislation is that nothing will make men work at an industry which does not pay as good a wage as they can earn in other equivalent employments; and if either employers or employed regard a decision as so unjust that they will rather fight than submit, it seems impossible to prevent a lock-out or a strike. According to Sir Henry Maine, elective government rests on the principle that we count heads simply to save the trouble of breaking them. But if the members of a minority would rather have their heads broken than submit, counting heads does not secure peace. Legislation for maintaining industrial peace is subject to the same limitations as elections in testing public opinion and Hague tribunals in averting international strife.

"*White Australia.*" The most urgent need of Australia is increased population. The population at the present time is only 1·53 per square mile. Australia could multiply its present population by securing immigrants from the teeming peoples of south-eastern Asia; and if it chose to avail itself of that source of labour various industries which are now impracticable could be established. It has been proved that some of the northern districts of Australia will grow cotton of first-rate quality; but cotton cannot be profitably cultivated without cheap labour for picking the crop. Hence under present conditions cotton cultivation in northern Australia is commercially impracticable. Australia holds that the evils of the intermixture of coloured with white people are so serious, that it is wise to make many sacrifices to maintain the whole continent as the home of a white race. It recognizes that this policy means that for the present certain industries cannot be established; but it considers that the advantages are well worth the delay. The experience of the Hawaian or Sandwich Islands shows the dangers of the unlimited introduction of oriental labour. Chinese and Japanese were introduced to supply unskilled work. They have increased until they furnish nine-tenths of the agricultural labour and have forced their way into the skilled crafts and mercantile work. The labour of the island has been completely orientalized—and without securing industrial peace.

It seems only fair, that if a coloured race be allowed to settle in a country, it should be allowed to enter any sphere of work. Otherwise those who may be physically weak but intellectually strong have no opportunity of earning their living. Australia, to avoid the fate of Hawaii, has resolved on a determined attempt to maintain the whole continent for the white race. The most serious conflict between Australia and the Empire was in regard to this policy.

Australia has restricted the influx of Asiatics by ingenious regulations, some of which had the opposite effect to that intended. Thus the Chinese were fast capturing the whole furniture manufacture. To stop this process, Victoria passed a law enacting that all furniture must be stamped with the name and address of its maker, so that purchasers might reject Chinese made goods. The dealers however objected to stocking furniture which was stamped with the name and address of a maker who was European in race; for their customers would simply buy from the manufacturer and save the shop-keepers' profit. The Chinese makers being less accessible, people were less likely to deal with them directly, and thus the shopkeepers preferred Chinese made goods.

The "White Australia policy" is faced by the

difficulty that northern Australia lies within the tropics, and though some of the tropical districts are dry and elevated, some of them, such as the coastal regions of Queensland, have an ultra-tropical climate. The proposal to develop tropical Australia by white labour is confronted by the deep conviction that this policy is unnatural, and that white people are physiologically unfitted for manual labour and colonisation in the tropics. The belief was long universal that the tropics are the natural home of the coloured races and the temperate regions of the white, and that the colour of the human skin is an adaptation to climate. Hence it was held that a white race settled in the tropics must degenerate. This view is, however, not really supported by the distribution of the white and coloured races. The one great fact in agreement with it is that the white section of mankind had its home in Europe and western Asia. Elsewhere colour and climate differ in distribution. America, from the Arctic to southern Patagonia, was occupied by one race, and its colour was as marked in the tribes living on the subantarctic coasts of Tierra del Fuego as in the tropics. The Maoris, living in the other southern-most of inhabited localities, are as brown as their cousins in the tropical islands of the Pacific. The yellow Mongolians range from the cold plains of Siberia to the tropical forests of Siam.

In recent years physiologists have been en-
deavouring to discover some physiological differences
between the white and the coloured races which
would explain why the former have found the tropics
so unhealthy. Many suggestions have been made,
but so far all have failed. The unhealthiness of the
tropics is now attributed to diseases, to which the
white man, being new to them, may be more sensitive
than the black. But these diseases are due to
parasitic organisms and not to climate, and there
appears to be no physiological reason why white
colonies should not be established in the tropics
provided that dwellings and habits be adjusted to
the local conditions.

Northern Queensland has furnished the best
example hitherto of a British colony in a tropical
land, and the Queensland coasts with their heavy
rainfall and moist air have extreme tropical charac-
teristics. Nevertheless the health statistics and the
experience of the schools in the tropical towns show
that the people are above the average in healthiness;
the expectation of life is longer there than in some of
the southern states of Australia, and the reports of
educational authorities and the tests of physiological
experts show that the children even of the third
generation, present no signs of either physical or
intellectual deterioration.

One of the chief products of Queensland is sugar

and it has often been maintained that sugar cultivation is the branch of tropical agriculture for which
white labour is least possible. The industry was
started in Australia with labour supplied by the
Kanakas, who are natives of the South Sea Islands.
The evils consequent on their advent and the difficulty of restricting them to the work for which they
were introduced led to the passing of an Act, in 1901,
prohibiting the entrance of any more Kanakas and
arranging for the repatriation of those already in the
country at the end of their then existing terms of
service.

It was confidently predicted that the expulsion of
the Kanakas meant the end of the Queensland sugar
industry; but Australia was so conscious of the evils
of a mixed population that it accepted the conclusion
that if the industry could only be maintained by
coloured labour, it had better cease. The sugar
industry was not then in a flourishing condition, but
its disappearance would have been a serious loss to
Queensland; nevertheless the expulsion of the
Kanakas was demanded most urgently by the
Queensland representatives in the Federal Parliament. The result is that with the exception of the
Kanakas who had married or made homes in
Australia before 1901, the whole of them have been
sent back to the Pacific islands. Instead of about
twelve per cent. of the sugar being grown by white

labour and eighty-eight per cent. by coloured labour, the figures are reversed. Nearly all the sugar now produced in Australia is grown by white labour, and instead of the industry having been ruined by the expulsion of the Kanakas it has continued to develop. Owing to the special conditions of sugar cultivation the changes in production from year to year are so great that there is no regular progress[1], but the area under cultivation and the tonnage of sugar produced have both increased since the industry has been made dependent on white labour.

The employment of white labour in the sugar plantations is one of the most daring of all Australian industrial experiments, and the statistics show that it has been crowned with success. It has shown, in spite of confident predictions to the contrary, that sugar can be profitably cultivated by white labour; and if white labour can do the hard manual toil in

[1] The sugar yield declined seriously in 1911 and 1912 owing to unfavourable seasons; but in 1913 the yield has recovered, as is shown by the following statistics quoted from *The Week* (Brisbane, 17th July, 1914):

Queensland	1912	1913	Increase in 1913
Output of sugar in tons ...	113,060	242,837	129,777
Output of cane in tons ...	994,212	2,085,588	1,091,376
Acres under cane ...	141,652	147,743	6,091
Acreage crushed ...	78,142	102,803	24,661
New South Wales			
Output of sugar in tons ...	16,733	22,573	5,840

these low-lying, humid sugar fields, there seems no
physical reason why white labour should not be
successfully employed in other branches of tropical
agriculture. The difficulty is financial not climatic.
It is probably true that white labour cannot compete
with coloured labour in a country occupied by a large
coloured population; but the great experiment in
the sugar industry has shown that where there is
no mixture of races white labour can do all the
necessary work. It has shown moreover that the
superior efficiency of the white labourer goes far
to annul and perhaps completely to annul the higher
nominal wages of the white man.

   Contract Labour.   It would however be no use
prohibiting the entrance of cheap coloured labour,
if the rates of white wages in Australia were cut
down by the unlimited entrance of people from
southern or eastern Europe who were brought in
under contract at a starvation wage. Australia
has accordingly followed the American example and
prohibited the import of unskilled labour under
contract. This policy led to a loud outcry against
the asserted refusal of Australia to allow the entrance
of newcomers. In order to prevent the unlimited
entrance of Asiatics the Immigration Acts gave
Australia the right to exclude any undesirable aliens
as well as unskilled labourers under contract. The
purpose of the regulations against the immigration

of unskilled labour under contract has been misunderstood in Great Britain. Wages in Australia are much higher than in southern Europe. A miner in some of the remoter fields in Australia may make in an eight hours shift more than an Italian peasant can earn in a week. Immigration agents might therefore persuade ignorant peasants from the south of Europe to go to Australia under agreements to work for wages which might seem magnificent, but would not be a living wage in some of the more expensive back-country mining towns. Hence the law prohibits the entrance of unskilled labourers under contract, so that it shall not be called upon to enforce unjust contracts made in ignorance. An unskilled labourer may enter Australia and there he will have the benefit of the advice of his consul and can discover for himself prices and the cost of living. Then he can make whatever legal contract he chooses. Skilled labourers are allowed to enter under contract, for it is assumed that they have sufficient knowledge to safeguard their own interests.

There is nothing in this legislation to discourage immigration; the recent Federal Labour Government has done more than any other to encourage immigration. All Australia demands is that the new comers shall be prepared to live and work up to Australian standards of comfort and efficiency.

CHAPTER XII

CONCLUSION

Australia is sometimes represented as a monotonous country, a fringe of inhabitable land round a useless desert; it has, it is said, a stagnant population because its gold mines no longer attract immigrants; its soil is easily exhausted; it is burdened with a debt of over £60 per head; it is tending to inevitable bankruptcy under the incompetent rule of a caucus of envious demagogues.

Facts present a totally different picture. Australia is a land of exceptional variety and beauty. Though the rainfall in the interior is low, yet owing to its seasonal distribution and the nature of the soil and climate, it can be used to the best advantage. The population is still quite inadequate, for Australia could no doubt maintain in comfort 100,000,000 people; yet considering its remote position Australia has done very well to have raised its population from 405,000 to 4,750,000 in about sixty years. Though the gold yield is diminishing, Australia has vast reserves of other minerals, including coal, iron ores, oil shale, and china clay, and the decrease from the gold mines is partly due to the fact that gold is the one product whose price cannot be raised by its producers. Gold-mining is the industry which is most seriously affected by a general rise in prices, as it cannot recompense itself for increased working costs by charging higher for its produce.

The productivity of Australia per head of population is unequalled. The resources of the country are immense. The debt though large is covered by the railways and other public works. And Australia instead of travelling down an easy road to ruin, is pursuing a strenuous, progressive policy, which is dictated by the highest ideals of citizenship.

The economic success of Australia would have been impossible had not the Australians faced their new problems with fearless confidence, and solved them by patient experiment, unusual originality, and unflinching thoroughness in work. These qualities have been shown by the pioneers in pastoral settlement, by its skilled sheep breeders, by the mining prospectors who discovered the Australian gold-fields, by the mining engineers who devised new methods of working the ores, and by the politicians who, animated by the same spirit, are resolute that the degrading poverty of the European and American slums shall find no home in Australia.

The characteristic which always seems to me the chief distinction of Australian politics is its dominant idealism. The Australian differs perhaps most strikingly from the American and Canadian by being more idealist and less romantic. The average American seems to me essentially a romanticist, for he is interested in the unusual because it is unusual. The Australian on the contrary is an idealist, for he does not care much for novelty unless it offers some prospect of improving present conditions. He shows in an especially strong degree that combination of the imaginative and the practical, which is the most marked characteristic of the British race.

The Australian is therefore not to be turned from his path by showing him that his measures for the benefit of his artisan class impoverish the country by delaying its development and enrichment. For much of the social legislation of Australia is based on the deliberate rejection of the view that financial success is any real test of national prosperity. The well known award by Mr Justice Higgins on the Broken Hill strike clearly expresses that principle. The miners demanded a wage which according to the employers the mine could not pay. The Judge estimated the lowest wage on which a man could be expected to live in reasonable comfort and maintain his health, with the prices and conditions ruling in that isolated expensive mining field. Having determined what he considered a living wage he declared that if the mine could not pay as much, it must close down until a rise in the price of metals or fall in local costs enabled the mine to give a living wage. It is fully recognized that the industrial and social legislation of Australia is to some extent raising the cost of production, is preventing the establishment of certain industries, and is restricting the growth of others. Australia adopted her present industrial policy fully prepared to pay the cost. The question is whether the financial handicap that has been accepted will seriously hamper the development of the continent. The statistics quoted in the previous pages show that Australia is making magnificent progress, and the fact that the price of Australian securities rose in Europe during the first Labour administration indicated that British capitalists had no real fear that Labour rule was any real menace to Australian progress.

The determination of Australia to secure the well-being of its working classes may reduce its wealth producing power; but that does not prove that the policy is unsound or even extravagant. It only shows that in contrast with the prevalent materialism of the time, Australia recognizes that it is the duty of a state to safeguard its citizens against intellectual as well as against bodily foes. Australia is striving to secure conditions which will foster the growth of a higher average standard of character than has been possible in the uneven and conflicting growths of the older nations. The prospects of success are hopeful.

The rough and tumble of back-bush life, the horse-play of the shearing shed, the taciturn melancholy of the shepherd of the central plains, the improvidence of the swagsman, and the coarse revel of the prospector seeking relief from a long spell of solitude, often obscure the real qualities of the Australian; and the apparently wasteful destruction of the forests when the land is cleared for the settler and the untidiness of the preliminary "bushwhacking" may give the impression that Australian methods are improvident and unfinished. But such a conclusion would be unjust, and no one can have come much across the Australian without recognizing his well justified self-reliance, versatile ingenuity and originality, steadfast loyalty to his comrades and his work, and constant readiness to invest his last shilling in opening a new mining field or to spend himself in redeeming a tract of virgin land. No one can fail to realize that a large share of Australia's glorious achievements has been won by the heroic privates in the industrial army of Australia.

SHORT BIBLIOGRAPHY

"The Federal Handbook prepared in connection with the......meeting of the British Association......in Australia, August, 1914" published by the Commonwealth Government includes contributions written by leading Australian authorities on the History, Geography, Fauna and Flora, Geology, Meteorology, Economics, and Educational and Political Systems of Australia.

This work is supplemented by excellent handbooks prepared for the same meeting by the states of New South Wales, Victoria, and Tasmania.

The leading contributions to the science of Australia are published in the journals of the Royal Societies of New South Wales, Victoria, South Australia, Queensland and Tasmania; of the Linnean Society of New South Wales; in the Records of the Australian Museum, Sydney, and in the publications of the Geological Survey of each of the States.

Statistics

Official Yearbook of the Commonwealth of Australia (No. 8, 1915).

History

BARTON, G. B., History of New South Wales, 1889–94.

JENKS, ED., History of the Australasian Colonies (3rd Edit., Cambridge University Press, 1912).

JOSE, A. W., Short History of Australasia, 1899.

MOORE, W. H., The Constitution of the Commonwealth of Australia, 1909.

PARKES, Sir H., Fifty Years in the making of Australian History, 1892.

TURNER, H. GYLES, History of Victoria, 1904.

WISE, B. R., The Making of the Australian Commonwealth, 1889–1900.

Geography

ROGERS, J. D., Historical Geography of Australia, 1907.

STANFORD'S Compendium of Geography, Australasia, Vol. I, 1907.

TAYLOR, T. G., Australia (Clarendon Press).

Exploration

COLLINGRIDGE, G., First Discovery of Australia, 1906. (This work contains reproductions of many early maps.)

FAVENC, E., History of Australian Exploration, 1888.

INDEX

www.ingramcontent.com/pod-product-compliance
Ingram Content Group UK Ltd.
Pitfield, Milton Keynes, MK11 3LW, UK
UKHW042145280225
455719UK00001B/105